THE ART OF LIVING

THE ART OF LIVING

Finding Purpose and Meaning in Life

B. VINCENT

QuantumQuill Press

Contents

I

Chapter 1: Introduction to Living with Purpose

Characterizing Reason and Significance

In the mind boggling woven artwork of human life, reason and importance act as directing strings, winding through the texture of our lives, imbuing every second with importance and course. Reason, the signal that enlightens our way, is the main thrust behind our activities, the compass that steers us toward satisfaction. The inborn inspiration powers our undertakings, pushing us to take a stab at more noteworthy levels and more profound comprehension.

Importance, then again, presents lavishness to our encounters, instilling them with importance and reverberation. The embodiment injects our collaborations, connections, and pursuits with profundity and importance, changing the commonplace into the remarkable. Together, reason and significance structure the foundation of an everyday routine very much experienced, giving an internal compass and satisfaction in the midst of the intricacies of presence.

To genuinely get a handle on the quintessence of direction and significance, it is fundamental to dive underneath the surface and investigate their nuanced complexities. Reason, frequently confounded as an elevated desire or bombastic objective, rises above simple accomplishment or achievement. It includes the arrangement of our activities with our qualities, the quest for tries that resound with our center convictions and yearnings.

Additionally, importance reaches out past shallow fulfillment or short lived joys, digging into the profundities of our essences. It emerges from snapshots of association, genuineness, and greatness, imbuing our lives with a feeling of importance and having a place. By understanding the transaction among reason and importance, we leave upon an excursion of self-disclosure and satisfaction, opening the potential for significant development and change.

In the sections that follow, we will investigate the bunch aspects of direction and significance, revealing their importance to our day to day routines and goals. Through thoughtfulness, reflection, and activity, we will set out upon a journey of self-revelation and strengthening, developing a more profound comprehension of our special reason and the significant importance it gives to our reality.

Significance of Carrying on with a Deliberate Life

In a world overflowing with interruptions and vulnerabilities, the quest for a deliberate life arises as a guide of lucidity in the midst of the confusion. Living with design isn't just an elevated ideal; it is a crucial part of human thriving, fundamental for opening our actual potential and tracking down satisfaction in our undertakings.

At its center, a deliberate life gives an internal compass and importance, directing our activities and decisions toward the main thing to us. It imbues our days with a feeling of importance, changing routine undertakings into significant commitments to a bigger vision. Without reason, we endanger floating randomly through life, without any trace of course and energy, surrendered to a destiny directed by situation as opposed to decision.

Besides, a deliberate life permeates us with flexibility despite difficulty, empowering us to endure life's hardships with beauty and assurance. When faced with difficulties or mishaps, people with an unmistakable feeling of direction are better prepared to continue on, drawing strength from their characteristic inspiration to conquer hindrances and move forward.

Besides, living with reason encourages a significant feeling of satisfaction and fulfillment, rising above the quest for outside approval or material achievement. Dissimilar to temporary delights or shallow accomplishments, the satisfaction got from adjusting our activities to our motivation is persevering and profoundly fulfilling, reverberating with the actual center of our being.

Significantly, embracing an intentional life helps the person as well as has far reaching influences that stretch out to the more extensive local area and society overall. By living genuinely and chasing after our interests, we motivate others to do likewise, making a far reaching influence of positive change and change.

Basically, the significance of carrying on with a deliberate life couldn't possibly be more significant. It is the foundation whereupon our feeling of satisfaction, flexibility, and effect rests. As we set out upon the excursion of self-revelation and reason, let us embrace the groundbreaking force of living with purposefulness, for in doing as such, we open the potential for an existence of importance, satisfaction, and significant importance.

Normal Confusions About Reason

Inside the woven artwork of human getting it, misinterpretations frequently dark the genuine substance of ideas, creating shaded areas where lucidity ought to rule. Reason, a reference point of direction and inspiration, isn't invulnerable to such confusions. Without a doubt, in the midst of the bunch understandings and presumptions, normal misinterpretations about reason proliferate, blurring our discernment and thwarting our quest for a deliberate life.

One predominant confusion is the thought that object is inseparable from a gaudy, particular objective or desire. While it is actually the case that reason can appear chasing huge accomplishments or achievements, it isn't restricted to such undertakings. Reason envelops the arrangement of our activities with our qualities, the quest for attempts that reverberate with our center convictions and yearnings, no matter what their scale or degree.

Another confusion is the conviction that design is static and constant, a proper objective to be reached as opposed to a powerful excursion of development and self-disclosure. In actuality, reason develops and unfurls over the long run, molded by our encounters, bits of knowledge, and reflections. It is a consistent course of investigation and refinement, expecting receptiveness to change and transformation.

Besides, there exists a misguided judgment that design is foreordained or forced upon us by outer powers, like cultural assumptions or familial tensions. While outside impacts without a doubt shape our impression of direction, genuine satisfaction emerges from adjusting our activities to our valid selves, producing a way that mirrors our novel qualities and desires.

Furthermore, there is a misinterpretation that design is exclusively tracked down in work or vocation pursuits, ignoring the heap different features of life where reason can show. Reason saturates each part of our reality, from our connections and leisure activities to our commitments to everyone's benefit. It isn't restricted to the domains of expert achievement yet stretches out to the domain of individual satisfaction and association.

In conclusion, there is a misguided judgment that object is an honor held for the lucky few, difficult to reach to those wrestling with misfortune or difficulty. Actually, reason can rise out of the most far-fetched of conditions, manufactured in the pot of difficulty and strength. It isn't subject to outer conditions yet dwells inside every one of us, ready to be uncovered and embraced.

In scattering these normal confusions about reason, we prepare for a more profound comprehension and enthusiasm for its actual quintessence. By perceiving reason as a dynamic, complex excursion of self-disclosure and development, we enable ourselves to live with purposefulness and significance, rising above the constraints of misguided judgment to embrace the endless conceivable outcomes that exist in.

Advantages of Tracking down Reason

In the embroidery of human life, reason fills in as a string that winds around together the dissimilar components of our lives, permeating them with importance and importance. Past simple existential ponderings, the quest for reason yields unmistakable advantages that improve our prosperity and upgrade our personal satisfaction.

Tracking down reason, most importantly, gives a significant internal compass and lucidity in exploring the intricacies of life. At the point when we adjust our activities to our qualities and yearnings, we graph a course that resounds with our true selves, directing us toward satisfaction and fulfillment. This feeling of direction fills in as a directing light in the midst of life's vulnerabilities, offering comfort and consolation in the midst of uncertainty or disarray.

Besides, living with reason cultivates a profound feeling of satisfaction and fulfillment that rises above transitory joys or shallow accomplishments. Dissimilar to the empty quest for material achievement or outside approval, the satisfaction got from living with design is persevering and profoundly fulfilling, resounding with the actual center of our being. This internal satisfaction powers our inspiration and versatility, engaging us to continue on notwithstanding affliction and seek after our fantasies with immovable assurance.

Besides, intentional living develops a significant feeling of association and having a place, both to ourselves and to our general surroundings. At the point when we live in arrangement with our motivation, we produce significant connections and add to everyone's benefit, making a feeling of solidarity and kinship that enhances our lives immensely. This feeling of having a place supports our spirits and encourages a profound feeling of satisfaction, building up our inherent worth and worth as individuals from the human family.

Moreover, living with reason improves our general prosperity and emotional wellness, diminishing pressure and nervousness while expanding flexibility and confidence. Research has shown that people who have a reasonable feeling of direction experience more noteworthy mental prosperity and are better outfitted to adapt to life's difficulties. Deliberate living gives a feeling of importance and soundness to our encounters, permitting us to explore life's high points and low points with effortlessness and flexibility.

Eventually, the advantages of finding reason reach out a long ways past the individual, enhancing our own carries on with as well as the existences of everyone around us. By living truly and chasing after our interests, we motivate others to do likewise, making a gradually expanding influence of positive change and change that resonates all through our networks and then some. In embracing the extraordinary force of direction, we open the potential for an existence of importance, bliss, and significant importance.

Making way for the Excursion Ahead

As we stand at the edge of self-disclosure and intentional living, it is crucial for made way for the groundbreaking excursion that lies ahead. The way to finding our motivation isn't only an objective to be reached however a significant odyssey of investigation and development, requiring boldness, purposefulness, and receptiveness to plausibility.

We, first and foremost, should develop a feeling of interest and self-reflection, embracing the potential chance to dive profound into the openings of our souls and psyches. This excursion of contemplation involves looking at our interests, values, and convictions, disentangling the layers of molding and assumption that might cloud our actual longings and desires. By focusing a light on our deepest insights, we lay the basis for uncovering our remarkable reason and producing a way that reverberates with our genuine selves.

Besides, we should develop a mentality of transparency and receptivity, remaining sensitive to the murmurs of instinct and motivation that guide us along our excursion. The quest for intention is definitely not a straight way yet a wandering journey of revelation, loaded up with exciting bends in the road, misfortunes and forward leaps. By embracing the vulnerability and uncertainty intrinsic in this excursion, we open ourselves to the endless potential outcomes that lie past our usual ranges of familiarity, permitting ourselves to be driven by the insight of our internal compass.

Besides, we should develop a feeling of responsibility and obligation to our own development and improvement. The excursion of deliberate living requires mental fortitude and flexibility despite difficulty, as well as an eagerness to face the feelings of trepidation and questions that might emerge en route. By considering ourselves responsible to our desires and responsibilities, we enable ourselves to conquer snags and difficulties, continuing onward with faithful assurance and resolve.

Moreover, we should develop a feeling of appreciation and appreciation for the endowments and potential open doors that encompass us. Appreciation opens our hearts and psyches to the wealth of life, cultivating a feeling of satisfaction and satisfaction that rises above material belongings or outside accomplishments. By developing a mentality of appreciation, we conform to the progression of overflow and plausibility, welcoming endowments and chances to appear in our lives.

At last, we should develop a feeling of association and having a place, perceiving that we are in good company on this excursion. As we leave upon the way of deliberate living, we hold hands with close allies and individual voyagers, joined by our common journey for importance and satisfaction. By encouraging strong connections and networks, we draw strength and motivation from each other, exploring the exciting bends in the road of the street ahead with elegance and flexibility.

In making way for the excursion ahead, we establish the groundwork for an existence of direction, significance, and satisfaction. By developing interest, receptiveness, responsibility, appreciation, and association, we set out upon a groundbreaking odyssey of self-revelation and development, opening the potential for significant delight, importance, and effect in our lives and our general surroundings.

2

Chapter 2: Self-Discovery

Investigating Your Interests and Interests

In the maze of self-revelation, our interests and interests act as directing stars, enlightening the way to an existence of direction and satisfaction. These are the pursuits that light our spirits, injecting every second with imperativeness and significance. However, in the midst of the rushing about of day to day existence, we might fail to focus on these fortunes, covered underneath layers of commitment and schedule.

To leave upon the excursion of self-revelation is to set out upon a journey of investigation, an odyssey into the profundities of our being. It starts with a basic inquiry: What gives you pleasure? Pause for a minute to contemplate this inquiry, permitting your psyche to meander unreservedly without judgment or imperative. Review the exercises and encounters that have mixed your interest and excitement, touching off a flash inside you.

Maybe it is the adventure of making workmanship with your hands, the invigoration of investigating new scenes, or the fulfillment of addressing complex riddles. Anything that structure it might take, your enthusiasm is an impression of your actual quintessence, a brief look into the profundities of your spirit. Carve out opportunity to investigate these interests, to submerge yourself completely in the exercises that give you pleasure, for it is inside these snapshots of stream and commitment that your motivation starts to uncover itself.

Also, consider the qualities and convictions that support your interests, the goals that resound with your center being. Do your inclinations line up with your most profound feelings and goals? Is it true or not that they are an impression of your legitimate self, or do they just reflect outer impacts and assumptions? By adjusting your interests to your qualities, you guarantee that your activities are as one with your actual reason, prompting an existence of more prominent legitimacy and satisfaction.

Chasing after self-disclosure, there are no off-base responses, no foreordained objections. It is an excursion of investigation and trial and error, a course of experimentation. Embrace the vulnerability and uncertainty of this excursion, permitting yourself to meander down surprising ways and find stowed away fortunes en route.

Keep in mind, your interests are not simple leisure activities or hobbies; they are the keys that open the way to your motivation. By investigating your inclinations with interest and receptiveness, you set up for an existence of significance and satisfaction, one where each second is injected with reason and bliss. Thus, hope against hope, try to investigate, for inside the profundities of your interests lies the key to opening your actual potential and carrying on with an existence of significant importance.

Considering Individual Qualities and Convictions

In the woven artwork of our lives, our qualities and convictions act as the dynamic strings that wind around together the texture of our reality. They are the core values that shape our choices, activities, and cooperations with our general surroundings. To set out upon the excursion of self-disclosure is to dig profound into the repository of our qualities and convictions, to uncover the crucial bits of insight that characterize what our identity is and a big motivator for we.

Pause for a minute to stop and ponder the qualities that resound profoundly inside your spirit. What standards do you hold dear? Respectability, sympathy, realness? Consider the standards that you endeavor to maintain in your day to day existence, the characteristics that you respect in others and try to exemplify yourself. These qualities are not simple reflections; they are the compass that directs your ethical compass, guiding you to an existence of direction and uprightness.

Also, think about the convictions that shape your view of the world and your place inside it. What bits of insight do you hold to be undeniable? Is it true or not that they are established in confidence, reason, or individual experience? Ponder the accounts and legends that have formed your perspective, the tales that you enlighten yourself regarding what your identity is and what you are prepared to do. Are these convictions serving you well, or would they say they are keeping you away from understanding your actual potential?

As you dig further into the maze of your qualities and convictions, be ready to face logical inconsistencies and irregularities inside yourself. Not a solitary one of us are great, and our qualities and convictions might develop and change after some time in light of new encounters and experiences. Embrace the course of self-assessment with lowliness and effortlessness, perceiving that development and self-revelation are progressing ventures, not limited objections.

In adjusting your activities to your qualities and convictions, you enable yourself to live with legitimacy and respectability, to walk your way with reason and conviction. At the point when your qualities are as one with your activities, you experience a significant feeling of arrangement and cognizance, a sensation of being consistent with yourself and your most profound yearnings.

Keep in mind, your qualities and convictions are the establishment whereupon your motivation is fabricated. By considering these center bits of insight with genuineness and earnestness, you lay the preparation for an existence of importance and satisfaction, one in which each choice and activity is directed by the illumination of your inward compass. Thus, find opportunity to investigate and embrace your qualities and convictions, for inside them lies the way to opening your actual potential and carrying on with an existence of direction and enthusiasm.

Evaluating Qualities and Shortcomings

In the embroidery of human life, every one of us has a novel exhibit of gifts, abilities, and capacities, woven along with our singular eccentricities and quirks. To leave upon the excursion of self-disclosure is to embrace a profound and legitimate evaluation of these qualities and shortcomings, to uncover the strings that characterize our substance and shape our true capacity.

Start by considering your assets, those inborn characteristics and capacities that put you aside and push you toward progress. What are you normally great at? What undertakings or exercises do you succeed in easily? Consider the commendations and input you have gotten from others, as well as the minutes when you have felt generally invigorated and locked in. These are the signs that highlight your novel assets and abilities, the gifts that you bring to the world.

Simultaneously, recognize your shortcomings and regions for development with modesty and self-empathy. What difficulties do you confront? What parts of yourself do you battle to acknowledge or embrace? Perceive that your shortcomings don't characterize you; they are essentially regions in which you have the chance to learn and develop. By dealing with these difficulties directly and looking for help when required, you can change your shortcomings into assets and grow your possible in new and surprising ways.

Also, consider the job that mentality plays in forming your view of assets and shortcomings. Do you move toward difficulties with a development outlook, seeing mishaps as any open doors for learning and improvement? Or on the other hand do you capitulate to a proper mentality, it are static and permanent to trust that your capacities? Develop an outlook of versatility and development, embracing difficulties as venturing stones on the way to personal growth and self-disclosure.

As you evaluate your assets and shortcomings, recall that you are a work underway, ceaselessly developing and extending your true capacity. Embrace the course of self-assessment with interest and receptiveness, commending your triumphs and gaining from your disappointments en route. By outfitting the force of mindfulness and self-acknowledgment, you engage yourself to live with validness and reason, completely embracing the special gifts and open doors that life brings to the table.

Eventually, your assets and shortcomings are not obstructions to be survived yet chances to be embraced. By embracing your assets and shortcomings with lowliness and self-sympathy, you open the potential for development and self-disclosure, preparing for an existence of importance and satisfaction. In this way, find opportunity to survey your assets and shortcomings with genuineness and truthfulness, for inside them lies the way to opening your actual potential and carrying on with an existence of direction and enthusiasm.

Understanding Previous Encounters and Illustrations Learned

In the embroidery of our lives, each string addresses a one of a kind encounter, woven together to frame the complex texture of our reality. To set out upon the excursion of self-revelation is to unwind these strings, to analyze the embroidered artwork of our previous encounters and concentrate the insight and bits of knowledge that exist in.

Start by thinking about huge achievements, difficulties, and wins in your day to day existence venture. What minutes stand apart as defining moments or essential occasions? Consider the illustrations you have gained from these encounters, the experiences acquired, and the development that has happened thus. Whether win or affliction, each experience has formed you in significant ways, shaping you into the individual you are today.

In addition, consider the examples and topics that arise as you analyze your previous encounters. Do you see repeating themes of conduct or thought? Are there sure circumstances or connections that trigger natural reactions or responses? By recognizing these examples, you gain significant understanding into your subliminal convictions and inspirations, enlightening regions for development and personal growth.

As you ponder your previous encounters, be aware of the narratives you inform yourself concerning what your identity is and what you are prepared to do. Are these accounts engaging and asserting, or do they support restricting convictions and self-question? Develop a mentality of self-sympathy and interest, moving toward your previous encounters with transparency and receptivity.

Moreover, consider the job that pardoning and appreciation play in forming your impression of the past. Are there minutes or occasions that you presently can't seem to completely pardon or delivery? Are there endowments or valuable open doors that you have ignored or underestimated? By developing a feeling of pardoning and appreciation, you free yourself from the weights of disdain and lament, holding nothing back from the groundbreaking force of mending and development.

At last, the excursion of self-revelation isn't tied in with choosing not to move on or regretting botched open doors; it is tied in with embracing the current second with clearness and aim. By getting it and coordinating the illustrations gained from your previous encounters, you engage yourself to live with realness and reason, completely embracing the special gifts and open doors that every second presents.

In this way, carve out opportunity to think about your previous encounters with trustworthiness and genuineness, for inside them lies the insight and understanding that will direct you on your excursion of self-disclosure. Embrace the examples learned, praise the triumphs won, and delivery the weights that never again serve you. For in the embroidery of your past lies the way to opening your actual potential and carrying on with an existence of direction and enthusiasm.

Developing Mindfulness as an Establishment for Reason

At the core of self-disclosure lies the excursion of mindfulness, a significant investigation of the profundities of our being that enlightens the way to reason and satisfaction. To set out upon this excursion is to dig into the openings of our cognizance, to focus a light on the shadows of our feelings of dread and wants, and to embrace the completion of our true selves.

Start by developing care and thoughtfulness as everyday works on, permitting yourself to stop and ponder your considerations, feelings, and sensations with interest and non-judgment. Notice the examples and propensities that emerge inside your brain, the accounts you inform yourself regarding what your identity is and what you are prepared to do. By noticing these examples with clearness and mindfulness, you gain knowledge into the inward functions of your mind, uncovering the subliminal convictions and inspirations that shape your view of the real world.

Also, embrace self-acknowledgment and sympathy as primary standards on your excursion of self-revelation. Perceive that you are an intricate and diverse being, meriting affection and figuring out, defects what not. Discharge the need to pass judgment or reprimand yourself for saw inadequacies or flaws, and on second thought, develop a feeling of generosity and compassion toward yourself as well as other people. By embracing yourself with genuine love and acknowledgment, you establish a sustaining climate wherein development and change can prosper.

As you extend your mindfulness, investigate the profundities of your internal scene with fortitude and weakness. Confront your feelings of trepidation and instabilities with trustworthiness and transparency, recognizing the pieces of yourself that you might have recently stayed away from or denied. By going up against these shadows with boldness and sympathy, you recover your power and free yourself from the chains of self-restricting convictions and ways of behaving.

Besides, perceive the interconnectedness of all creatures and your general surroundings, developing a feeling of solidarity and having a place that rises above the limits of the singular self. By perceiving the inborn reliance of all life, you extend your mindfulness past the bounds of the inner self and embrace a more extensive point of view that envelops the prosperity of every conscious being.

At last, mindfulness is the foundation whereupon the structure of direction is assembled. By developing care, self-acknowledgment, and empathy, you establish the groundwork for an existence of importance and satisfaction, one where each second is saturated with lucidity, legitimacy, and reason. Thus, embrace the excursion of self-disclosure with boldness and interest, for inside the profundities of your own being lies the way to opening your actual potential and carrying on with an existence of significant importance.

3

Chapter 3: Clarifying Your Vision

Laying out Objectives Lined up with Your Qualities

In the tremendous span of human potential, objectives act as directing stars, enlightening the way toward a future saturated with reason and satisfaction. However, the simple quest for objectives isn't sufficient; they should be established in a groundwork of values and rules that resound profoundly inside our spirits. To set out upon the excursion of explaining our vision is to defined objectives that line up with our center convictions and desires, it are significant and deliberate to guarantee that our undertakings.

Start by considering the qualities and rules that are mean quite a bit to you. What goals do you hold dear? Trustworthiness, empathy, realness? Consider how these qualities illuminate your choices and activities, forming the manner in which you explore the world and connect with others. These qualities are the bedrock whereupon your objectives are constructed, giving a solid groundwork whereupon to fabricate your vision for what's to come.

Then, consider the desires and targets that line up with your qualities and standards. What do you expect to accomplish in your life? What dreams do you hold onto in the profundities of your spirit? Whether it's chasing after a significant vocation, developing profound and satisfying connections, or having a beneficial outcome on the world, your objectives ought to mirror your valid longings and add to your feeling of direction and satisfaction.

As you put forth your objectives, be aware of the significance of arrangement between your qualities and your activities. Guarantee that your objectives are not only shallow or remotely determined however are established in a profound comprehension of what your identity is and a big motivator for you. At the point when your objectives are lined up with your qualities, you experience a significant feeling of rationality and honesty, realizing that each step you take is together as one with your actual self.

Also, consider the effect that your objectives will have on your general prosperity and satisfaction. Is it true or not that they are helpful for an existence of equilibrium and completeness, or do they focus on one part of your life to the detriment of others? Endeavor to define objectives that include all components of your being - physical, close to home, mental, and otherworldly - guaranteeing that your quest for progress is comprehensive and economical.

At last, laying out objectives lined up with your qualities isn't simply a necessary evil yet an excursion of self-disclosure and self-articulation. By adjusting your objectives to your most profound yearnings and standards, you inject your existence with reason and significance, preparing for a future loaded up with satisfaction and bliss. In this way, hope against hope strikingly, set out to define objectives that resound with your spirit, for inside them lies the way to opening your actual potential and carrying on with an existence of significant importance.

Envisioning Your Optimal Life

In the immense material of presence, the force of creative mind fills in as a strong brush, painting the distinctive tones of our fantasies and goals onto the texture of the real world. To explain our vision is to leave upon an excursion of representation, to outfit the imaginative power inside us to imagine the existence we wish to lead with lucidity and conviction.

Start by making a safe-haven of quietness and peacefulness, a space where you can withdraw from the clamor and interruptions of the rest of the world and interface with the profundities of your creative mind. Shut your eyes and permit your brain to meander openly, free by the requirements of rationale or reason. Imagine the existence you wish to lead, permitting your creative mind to invoke pictures of your optimal reality with striking subtlety and lucidity.

Imagine each part of your life - your profession, your connections, your wellbeing, your relaxation exercises - with lively lucidity and force. See yourself flourishing in your picked calling, having a significant effect on the planet and making progress in your own particular manner. Experience the glow and association of profound and satisfying connections, encompassed by friends and family who backing and inspire you on your excursion. Envision yourself dynamic and brilliant, spilling over with wellbeing and essentialness, taking part in exercises that support your body, psyche, and soul.

As you submerge yourself in the profundities of your creative mind, permit yourself to encounter the feelings and sensations related with your optimal existence with full power. Feel the thrill of accomplishment, the glow of affection, the tranquility of internal harmony. Allow these sentiments to wash over you like a wave, injecting each fiber of your being with a feeling of delight, satisfaction, and appreciation.

Besides, use perception procedures to build up your vision and anchor it solidly in your psyche mind. Make vision sheets, montages, or diaries loaded up with pictures and words that address your optimal life, permitting them to act as day to day tokens of your yearnings and objectives. Practice perception practices routinely, envisioning yourself carrying on with your optimal existence with all the enthusiasm and force of a striking dream.

By bridling the force of perception, you enable yourself to show your fantasies and goals with clearness and reason. Representation fills in as an extension between the domain of creative mind and the domain of the real world, permitting you to rejuvenate your vision with goal and concentration. Thus, hope against hope strongly, set out to envision your optimal existence with steady conviction, for inside the profundities of your creative mind lies the way to opening your actual potential and carrying on with an existence of significant importance.

Distinguishing Snags and Difficulties

Chasing after our fantasies and yearnings, it is unavoidable that we will experience snags and difficulties en route. To explain our vision is to go up against these possible obstructions with fortitude and prescience, to expect the obstacles that might hinder our advancement and foster procedures to really conquer them.

Start by checking out the likely snags and difficulties that might emerge on your excursion toward understanding your vision. Think about both outside factors, like monetary requirements, strategic difficulties, or cultural standards, as well as inner obstructions, like self-question, feeling of dread toward disappointment, or restricting convictions. By focusing a light on these likely difficulties, you enable yourself to face them with clearness and strength.

Then, consider the methodologies and assets that you can use to conquer these obstructions and explore difficulties actually. Draw upon your assets, gifts, and capacities, as well as the help and direction of other people who have confronted comparative difficulties. Develop an outlook of versatility and genius, seeing impediments as any open doors for development and advancing as opposed to unfavorable hindrances.

Additionally, adjust and change your methodology because of changing conditions and unanticipated difficulties. Adaptability is a critical fixing in the recipe for progress, permitting you to turn and course-right depending on the situation while remaining consistent with your definitive vision and objectives. Embrace the vulnerability and vagueness of the excursion, realizing that every hindrance you experience is a venturing stone on the way to understanding your vision.

As you recognize hindrances and difficulties, likewise consider the job that dread plays in forming your view of them. Are your apprehensions in view of objective worries or unreasonable tensions? Could it be said that they are established in previous encounters or future projections? By focusing a light on the shadows of dread, you decrease their control over you and gain the mental fortitude to push ahead with certainty and conviction.

Eventually, the excursion of explaining your vision is certainly not a smooth and direct way yet a winding street loaded up with exciting bends in the road, highs and lows. By recognizing impediments and difficulties with lucidity and foreknowledge, you engage yourself to explore the excursion with effortlessness and flexibility, realizing that every hindrance you conquer carries you one bit nearer to understanding your vision. Thus, set out to go up against the difficulties that lie ahead with boldness and assurance, for inside the pot of difficulty lies the chance for development, change, and at last, the satisfaction of your most profound desires.

Making a Guide for Progress

Chasing our fantasies and goals, a reasonable guide fills in as our directing compass, coordinating our means toward the acknowledgment of our vision. To explain our vision is to graph a course for progress, framing noteworthy stages and achievements that will lead us nearer to our objectives with reason and aim.

Start by separating your overall vision into more modest, sensible objectives that are lined up with your qualities and goals. Consider the particular results you desire to accomplish and the means expected to contact them. By separating your vision into scaled down lumps, you make it more substantial and attainable, decreasing overpower and expanding inspiration.

Then, focus on your objectives in view of their significance and direness, zeroing in on those that will greatestly affect your general vision. Consider the assets and backing expected to accomplish every objective and foster a course of events for fulfillment. Set sensible cutoff times and achievements to keep yourself responsible and on target.

Besides, consider the possible obstructions and difficulties that might emerge on your excursion toward every objective, and foster alternate courses of action to really address them. Expect likely barricades and mishaps, and conceptualize elective techniques for defeating them. By getting ready for obstructions ahead of time, you engage yourself to explore them with beauty and versatility.

As you make your guide for progress, likewise consider the significance of equilibrium and prosperity in accomplishing your objectives. Guarantee that your objectives incorporate all parts of your life - physical, close to home, mental, and otherworldly - and focus on taking care of oneself and self-sympathy en route. Recollect that achievement isn't just about accomplishing outer achievements, however about carrying on with a day to day existence that is satisfying and significant on all levels.

At long last, be adaptable and versatile in your methodology, able to change your guide on a case by case basis in light of changing conditions and unanticipated difficulties. Embrace the iterative idea of the excursion, realizing that each step you take carries you nearer to your definitive vision, regardless of whether the way might wander aimlessly en route.

By making a guide for progress that is grounded in lucidity, expectation, and adaptability, you engage yourself to explore the excursion of understanding your vision with certainty and reason. Thus, hope against hope intensely, try to define objectives that move and challenge you, and set out to diagram a course toward a future loaded up with plausibility and commitment. For inside the profundities of your vision lies the plan for an existence of satisfaction, reason, and significant importance.

Focusing on an Unmistakable Vision for Your Future

In the embroidery of our fantasies and goals, clearness of vision fills in as the twist and weft, winding around together the strings of our expectations and wants into a firm and convincing image representing things to come we wish to make. To explain our vision is to distil our goals into their most flawless quintessence, to focus on the directing star that will enlighten our way and push us forward with reason and conviction.

Start by pondering the experiences acquired through the course of objective setting, perception, and guide creation. Consider the subjects and examples that rise up out of these activities, as well as the feelings and sensations evoked by your vision representing things to come. Focus on the inward stirrings of your spirit, the murmurs of instinct and motivation that guide you toward your most profound cravings and desires.

As you refine and explain your vision, endeavor to distil it into an unmistakable and convincing explanation that typifies the quintessence of what you desire to accomplish. Use language that is clear and suggestive, portraying the future you wish to make to your eye. Permit yourself to think beyond practical boundaries and reach skyward, embracing the unfathomable potential outcomes that exist in the profundities of your creative mind.

Besides, guarantee that your vision is lined up with your qualities, goals, and qualities, mirroring the quintessence of what your identity is and a big motivator for you. Consider how your vision adds to your feeling of direction and satisfaction, as well as its possible effect on your general surroundings. At the point when your vision is lined up with your most profound longings and yearnings, you experience a significant feeling of reverberation and lucidity, realizing that each step you take is to support your definitive reason.

As you focus on your unmistakable vision for the future, likewise let go of connections to explicit results and embrace the excursion of vulnerability and plausibility. Perceive that the way to understanding your vision might be loaded up with exciting bends in the road, promising and less promising times, and that diversions and misfortunes are an unavoidable piece of the excursion. Trust in the insight of your instinct and the direction of your internal compass, realizing that each step you take carries you nearer to your final location.

Eventually, explaining your vision for what's to come isn't just about defining objectives and making arrangements; it is tied in with taking advantage of the most profound profundities of your being and conforming to the most noteworthy articulation of what your identity is. By focusing on a reasonable vision that resounds with your spirit, you engage yourself to live with expectation, reason, and energy, making a daily existence that is loaded up with importance, satisfaction, and significant importance. In this way, hope against hope strikingly, try to explain your vision with resolute conviction, and set out to step strongly into the future that looks for you. For inside the profundities of your vision lies the commitment of an everyday routine that is genuinely worth experiencing.

4

Chapter 4: Overcoming Obstacles

Embracing Flexibility and Persistence

In the cauldron of life's difficulties, versatility arises as the resolute buddy that brings us through the most obscure of times and drives us toward the illumination of trust and probability. To beat impediments is to embrace flexibility and constancy as core values on our excursion, perceiving that difficulties are not barricades but rather reroutes that lead us toward more prominent strength and intelligence.

Start by developing a mentality of versatility, perceiving that difficulty is an inescapable piece of the human experience. Instead of review misfortunes as unfavorable snags, consider them to be open doors for development and learning. Embrace the difficulties that come your direction with mental fortitude and assurance, realizing that each obstacle you beat carries you one bit nearer to your objectives.

In addition, foster methodologies to return from difficulty and continue on even with difficulties. Draw upon your inward holds of solidarity and strength, taking advantage of the force of positive reasoning and self-conviction. Develop a feeling of confidence and trust, knowing that even in the most obscure of times, there is consistently a gleam of light holding back to direct you forward.

As you explore the promising and less promising times of life's excursion, make sure to be delicate with yourself and practice self-empathy. Recognize the challenges you face with generosity and understanding, and commend your flexibility and persistence notwithstanding affliction. By treating yourself with empathy and effortlessness, you establish a sustaining climate wherein versatility can thrive.

Besides, look for motivation from the people who have defeated apparently unrealistic chances and arose more grounded on the opposite side. Encircle yourself with accounts of versatility and win, drawing strength from the instances of other people who have confronted difficulty with boldness and beauty. Recollect that you are in good company on this excursion, and that there is a huge repository of help and consolation accessible to you.

Eventually, embracing flexibility and tirelessness isn't just about conquering deterrents; it is tied in with embracing the completion of existence with mental fortitude and conviction. By developing flexibility notwithstanding misfortune, you enable yourself to explore life's difficulties with effortlessness and pride, knowing that with every difficulty, you develop further and stronger. In this way, try to embrace strength as your unfaltering friend on the excursion of life, for inside its hug lies the ability to defeat any obstruction and arise triumphant on the opposite side.

Developing a Development Outlook

In the midst of the recurring pattern of life's difficulties, our outlook arises as a strong power that shapes our reaction to misfortune. Despite hindrances, developing a development outlook becomes principal, as it engages us to see mishaps not as disappointments but rather as any open doors for learning and development. This groundbreaking point of view permits us to explore difficulties with flexibility and positive thinking, encouraging a feeling of organization and strengthening notwithstanding difficulty.

Embrace the central standards of a development mentality, grasping that knowledge, ability, and capacities are not fixed qualities but rather can be created through devotion and exertion. Instead of survey mishaps as impressions of innate constraints, consider them to be brief obstructions on the way toward dominance and achievement. By moving your concentration from results to the method involved with learning and improvement, you open the potential for endless development and advancement.

Besides, praise progress and exertion over flawlessness, perceiving that the excursion of self-improvement is set apart by steady advances and continuous improvement. Embrace the force of yet, understanding that even despite starting mishaps or disappointments, there exists the potential for development and outcome later on. Develop a feeling of interest and versatility, moving toward difficulties with a feeling of trial and error and investigation.

As you develop a development mentality, encircle yourself with steady impacts that build up and urge your obligation to learning and development. Search out tutors, mentors, and companions who exemplify the standards of versatility and determination, drawing motivation from their model. Make a steady local area of similar people who inspire and support each other on the excursion toward individual and expert development.

Besides, practice self-reflection and care as devices for developing a development outlook. Carve out opportunity to think about your encounters and concentrate illustrations and experiences from the two triumphs and disappointments. Develop care practices like contemplation and journaling to develop mindfulness and profound versatility, empowering you to explore difficulties with lucidity and self-restraint.

At last, developing a development outlook isn't just about defeating hindrances; it is tied in with embracing the excursion of self-revelation and self-awareness with boldness and versatility. By embracing a development outlook, you enable yourself to explore life's difficulties with beauty and assurance, knowing that with every misfortune, you develop further and stronger. Thus, try to embrace the extraordinary force of a development outlook, for inside its hug lies the potential for limitless learning, development, and satisfaction.

Looking for Help and Direction

In the maze of life's difficulties, the excursion becomes lighter and more reasonable when we permit ourselves to rest on the mainstays of help and direction that encompass us. To beat snags is definitely not a singular undertaking however a cooperative exertion, improved by the insight, consolation, and friendship of the individuals who stroll close by us.

Contact companions, family, tutors, and mentors for help and direction during testing times. Encircle yourself with people who elevate and rouse you, who have faith in your true capacity and urge you to drive forward notwithstanding affliction. Share your battles and wins transparently and truly, permitting yourself to be helpless and open to the insight and bits of knowledge of others.

Make a strong local area of similar people who share your qualities and desires, who comprehend the difficulties you face and proposition sympathy and support en route. Develop profound and significant associations with the individuals who commend your victories and proposition a shoulder to rest on during troublesome times. Together, you can face the hardships of existence with mental fortitude and versatility, realizing that you are in good company on this excursion.

In addition, search out tutors and mentors who can offer direction and astuteness in light of their own encounters and ability. Search for people who have confronted comparable difficulties and conquered them with elegance and assurance, and draw motivation from their model. Search out open doors for mentorship and direction, whether through conventional training programs, organizing occasions, or special interactions.

As you look for help and direction, make sure to respond the thoughtfulness and liberality of others by giving your own help and consolation as a trade off. Listen attentively, offer inspirational statements, and offer your own bits of knowledge and encounters with the people who might battle. By building a culture of help and correspondence, you make a local area that blossoms with common regard and strengthening.

At last, looking for help and direction is certainly not an indication of shortcoming however a show of solidarity and insight. By permitting yourself to rest on the mainstays of help that encompass you, you engage yourself to explore life's difficulties with elegance and flexibility, realizing that you are in good company on this excursion. Thus, try to connect and rest on the help and direction of others, for inside their hug lies the strength and boldness to beat any deterrent that holds you up.

Rehearsing Taking care of oneself and Self-Empathy

In the persistent buzzing about of present day life, it's not difficult to neglect to focus on our own prosperity in the midst of the tumult of contending requests and assumptions. However, in the midst of the commotion of outside pressures, it is urgent to focus on taking care of oneself and self-sympathy as basic points of support for exploring life's snags with elegance and versatility.

Focus on taking care of oneself as a fundamental part of your day to day daily schedule, supporting your physical, close to home, and mental prosperity with aim and care. Set aside a few minutes for exercises that support your body, like activity, smart dieting, and satisfactory rest. Take part in rehearses that advance close to home prosperity, for example, journaling, contemplation, or investing energy in nature. Develop leisure activities and interests that give you pleasure and satisfaction, permitting yourself to re-energize and restore in the midst of life's difficulties.

Besides, practice self-empathy for of supporting a delicate and sustaining relationship with yourself, particularly during seasons of trouble and difficulty. Indulge yourself with thoughtfulness and understanding, recognizing the intrinsic mankind in committing errors and confronting difficulties. Offer yourself the very sympathy and empathy that you would stretch out to a dear companion or cherished one, perceiving that self-empathy isn't an extravagance however a need for exploring life's promising and less promising times with elegance and flexibility.

As you focus on taking care of oneself and self-empathy, be aware of the significance of defining limits and expressing no to exercises or responsibilities that channel your energy or undermine your prosperity. Figure out how to pay attention to your body and instinct, regarding your own necessities and constraints with empathy and regard. By focusing on taking care of oneself and self-sympathy, you make a strong groundwork whereupon to explore life's deterrents with elegance and flexibility.

Moreover, develop a feeling of appreciation and appreciation for you as well as your excursion, perceiving the intrinsic worth and nobility in being human. Commend your triumphs and achievements, regardless of how little, and recognize the headway you have made on your excursion of self-improvement and advancement. By developing a feeling of appreciation and self-appreciation, you sustain a feeling of flexibility and inward strength that will bring you through even extremely testing times.

Eventually, rehearsing taking care of oneself and self-empathy isn't egotistical or liberal however a demonstration of self-conservation and self confidence. By focusing on your own prosperity and supporting a delicate and humane relationship with yourself, you enable yourself to explore life's obstructions with effortlessness and flexibility, realizing that you deserve love and care. Thus, try to focus on taking care of oneself and self-sympathy as fundamental parts of your excursion, for inside their hug lies the strength and versatility to conquer any deterrent that holds you up.

Tracking down An open door in Misfortune

In the woven artwork of life, difficulty frequently arises as the pot where our personality is manufactured and our flexibility is tried. However, in the midst of the hardships of life's difficulties, lies the secret potential for development, change, and significant understanding. To beat hindrances isn't only to persevere through difficulty yet to embrace the chance for development and self-disclosure that they present.

Rethink hindrances as any open doors for development and change, perceiving that each challenge you face holds inside it the seeds of probability and reestablishment. Rather than survey misfortunes as unconquerable barricades, consider them to be solicitations to investigate new viewpoints, foster new abilities, and develop inward assets that will work well for you on your excursion.

Search for silver linings and secret gifts amidst difficulty, and use them as fuel to push you forward on your excursion. Maybe a difficulty in your profession makes the way for investigate new open doors or seek after a long-held energy. Perhaps a relationship challenge prompts you to develop your mindfulness and relational abilities, cultivating further associations with others. By rethinking difficulty as a chance for development, you engage yourself to explore life's difficulties with elegance and flexibility.

Besides, embrace the course of transformation and recharging that rises out of confronting impediments with fortitude and strength. Like a phoenix coming to life, permit yourself to rise up out of difficulty more grounded, smarter, and stronger than previously. Embrace the examples gained from your encounters and use them to illuminate your choices and activities pushing ahead.

As you explore life's obstructions, make sure to develop a feeling of interest and receptiveness, moving toward difficulties with a feeling of marvel and investigation. Embrace vulnerability and uncertainty, knowing that inside the profundities of the obscure untruths the potential for revelation and development. By embracing the excursion of development and change, you enable yourself to explore life's impediments with elegance and versatility, realizing that every difficulty isn't a loss however a venturing stone on the way toward your definitive predetermination.

Eventually, finding an amazing open door in difficulty isn't just about defeating impediments; it is tied in with embracing the completion of existence with boldness and strength, realizing that inside each challenge lies the potential for development and self-disclosure. In this way, try to embrace difficulty as an impetus for development and change, for inside its hug lies the ability to open your actual potential and carry on with an existence of significant importance.

Chapter 5: Cultivating Meaningful Relationships

Fabricating Profound Associations

In the mind boggling embroidery of human experience, connections stand as the energetic strings that wind around together the texture of our lives. Developing significant associations isn't simply a question of possibility; it requires expectation, exertion, and a profound obligation to supporting bonds in view of common regard, trust, and understanding.

Start by encouraging real associations grounded in validity and earnestness. Move toward your collaborations with others with an open heart and a readiness to embrace weakness. Share your considerations, sentiments, and encounters transparently, welcoming others to do likewise. By developing a space of credibility and straightforwardness, you establish the groundwork for profound and significant associations that rise above triviality and misrepresentation.

Besides, develop sympathy and empathy in your collaborations, looking to comprehend and uphold others on their excursion. Carve out opportunity to listen profoundly to the tales and encounters of people around you, offering sympathy and approval for their delights, distresses, and battles. Offer empathy and grace in a way that would sound natural to you and activities, stretching out some assistance to those out of luck and commending the victories and accomplishments of others with veritable energy.

As you fabricate profound associations, focus on higher standards when in doubt, zeroing in on sustaining a couple of significant connections as opposed to extending yourself far across an immense organization of colleagues. Put your significant investment in developing associations with people who share your qualities, interests, and goals, and who elevate and move you to be your best self.

Besides, perceive the significance of correspondence in building significant associations. Develop a feeling of liberality and giving, offering backing, generosity, and consolation to others without anticipating anything consequently. Simultaneously, be available to getting backing and consideration from others, permitting yourself to rest on your friends and family in the midst of hardship and weakness.

Eventually, constructing profound associations isn't just about enhancing our own lives; it is tied in with making a feeling of having a place and interconnectedness that supports the spirit and elevates the soul. By putting resources into bona fide connections in view of shared regard, trust, and understanding, you enhance your life vastly, making an organization of help and friendship that supports you through life's highs and lows. Thus, try to develop profound associations with others, for inside the hug of significant connections lies the genuine extravagance and excellence of the human experience.

Supporting Correspondence

In the orchestra of human association, correspondence fills in as the melodic hold back that fits our connections, cultivating figuring out, sympathy, and closeness. Developing significant associations expects us to support correspondence channels that work with open exchange, undivided attention, and real association.

Practice undivided attention as a central expertise in supporting correspondence inside your connections. Move toward discussions with a certified interest and an eagerness to hear and comprehend the points of view of others genuinely. Listen with your ears, yet with your heart, looking to feel for the feelings and encounters behind the words. By offering your full presence and consideration, you make a space where others feel esteemed, heard, and comprehended.

Besides, focus on transparent correspondence in your connections, making a place of refuge for weakness and credibility. Share your contemplations, sentiments, and goals straightforwardly and straightforwardly, welcoming others to do likewise. Participate in troublesome discussions with mental fortitude and sympathy, tending to clashes and worries with compassion and regard. By cultivating open correspondence channels, you set out open doors for developing closeness and association inside your connections.

As you support correspondence, focus on nonverbal signals and nonverbal communication, perceiving that a lot of correspondence happens past the expressed word. Be sensitive to unpretentious changes in tone, looks, and motions, involving them as important wellsprings of knowledge into the considerations and sensations of others. By leveling up your abilities of nonverbal correspondence, you improve your capacity to associate genuinely and empathically with everyone around you.

Moreover, practice emphatic correspondence for of communicating your necessities, limits, and wants with clearness and certainty. Self-assuredness permits you to advocate for you as well as your connections while regarding the independence and limits of others. Talk your reality with boldness and conviction, realizing that your voice matters and that true correspondence is fundamental for encouraging sound and satisfying connections.

At last, supporting correspondence isn't just about trading words; it is tied in with encouraging figuring out, sympathy, and association inside our connections. By developing open discourse, undivided attention, and decisive correspondence, you make an establishment for extending closeness and building entrust with those you love. In this way, set out to sustain correspondence inside your connections, for inside the force of credible association lies the genuine sorcery and excellence of human association.

Cultivating Correspondence

In the dance of connections, correspondence arises as the smooth three step dance that ties people together in an amicable organization of shared regard, backing, and appreciation. Developing significant associations involves cultivating a feeling of correspondence, where the two players add to the relationship's development and prosperity, encouraging a feeling of equilibrium and concordance.

Develop a feeling of liberality and giving inside your connections, offering backing, graciousness, and support to everyone around you without anticipating anything consequently. Stretch out some assistance to others in their critical crossroads, commending their triumphs and accomplishments with certified excitement and happiness. By typifying a feeling of liberality and giving, you make a climate of warmth and generosity that supports the obligations of association and cultivates a feeling of having a place.

Simultaneously, be available to getting backing and generosity from others, permitting yourself to rest on your friends and family in the midst of hardship and weakness. Perceive that tolerant assistance is certainly not an indication of shortcoming however an exhibition of trust and weakness, fortifying the obligations of association and extending closeness inside your connections. By permitting others to help you in your critical crossroads, you set out open doors for correspondence and common development inside your connections.

Besides, perceive the worth of common regard and appreciation in cultivating correspondence inside your connections. Praise the novel commitments and viewpoints of every person, recognizing the qualities and abilities they offer that would be useful. Offer thanks and appreciation for the help and benevolence you get from others, encouraging a culture of appreciation and affirmation inside your connections.

As you develop correspondence inside your connections, be aware of the significance of keeping up with equilibrium and limits. Abstain from falling into examples of over-giving or over-getting, perceiving that sound connections flourish with a feeling of equilibrium and balance. Convey transparently and genuinely with your friends and family about your necessities, limits, and assumptions, encouraging a feeling of shared understanding and regard.

At last, encouraging correspondence inside your connections isn't just about giving and getting; it is tied in with making a feeling of shared liability and common consideration that enhances the obligations of association and fortifies the texture of your connections. In this way, try to develop correspondence inside your connections, for inside its hug lies the genuine sorcery and magnificence of significant associations.

Settling Clashes with Empathy

In the embroidery of connections, clashes unavoidably emerge as a characteristic outcome of varying points of view, needs, and wants. In any case, the genuine trial of a significant association lies not in that frame of mind of contention but rather in the capacity to explore conflicts with sympathy, compassion, and shared regard. Developing significant connections involves creating successful compromise abilities that cultivate figuring out, mending, and development.

Move toward clashes with sympathy and empathy, trying to grasp the basic requirements, feelings, and viewpoints of all gatherings included. Develop a feeling of interest and transparency, welcoming exchange and investigation instead of preventiveness and fault. Practice undivided attention and approval, recognizing the feelings and encounters of others with sympathy and regard. By cultivating sympathy and empathy, you establish a protected and strong climate for tending to clashes and tracking down commonly useful arrangements.

Also, practice powerful compromise procedures that advance comprehension and cooperation instead of acceleration and aggression. Use strategies like undivided attention, summarizing, and reflecting to guarantee that all gatherings feel appreciated and comprehended. Cultivate open discourse and straightforwardness, empowering every person to offer their viewpoints, sentiments, and needs transparently and truly. Look for shared conviction and shared objectives, cooperating to find savvy fixes that address the basic worries of all gatherings included.

As you explore clashes inside your connections, focus on the protection of the relationship and the prosperity of all gatherings included. Perceive that clashes are valuable open doors for development and realizing, where misconceptions can be explained, connections can be reinforced, and more profound degrees of closeness can be produced. Move toward clashes with modesty and empathy, perceiving that not even one of us are awesome and that we as a whole commit errors. By stretching out elegance and pardoning to ourselves as well as other people, we set out open doors for mending and compromise inside our connections.

Moreover, look for outside help and direction when clashes become overpowering or settled in. Think about enrolling the assistance of a confided in companion, relative, or specialist to give point of view and direction on the best way to explore the difficulties you face. Perceive that looking for help is an indication of solidarity, not shortcoming, and that there is intelligence and understanding to be acquired according to the points of view of others.

Eventually, settling clashes with sympathy isn't just about tracking down answers for explicit conflicts; it is tied in with developing figuring out, reinforcing bonds, and encouraging a culture of compassion and regard inside our connections. Thus, try to move toward clashes with empathy and modesty, for inside the pot of contention lies the chance for development, recuperating, and more profound association.

Putting resources into Development and Shared Encounters

In the nursery of connections, development thrives when supported by the ripe soil of shared encounters and common desires. Developing significant associations requires a promise to individual and aggregate development, as well as a readiness to put resources into shared exercises and encounters that extend bonds and make enduring recollections.

Focus on self-awareness inside your connections, supporting each other's goals and encouraging a feeling of consistent learning and improvement. Urge each other to seek after interests, interests, and objectives that carry satisfaction and importance to your lives. Praise each other's accomplishments and achievements, offering backing and support en route. By putting resources into one another's development and prosperity, you make an establishment for extending closeness and association inside your connections.

In addition, put resources into shared encounters and significant exercises that cultivate association and make enduring recollections together. Whether it's investigating new spots, attempting new leisure activities, or setting out on undertakings together, shared encounters give amazing chances to holding, chuckling, and happiness. Focus on quality time spent together, liberated from interruptions and commitments, where you can interface on a more profound level and fortify the obligations of closeness and kinship.

As you put resources into development and shared encounters inside your connections, be aware of the significance of correspondence and coordinated effort. Look for input from one another on exercises and encounters that reverberate with your common advantages and values, and be available to attempting new things together. Split the difference and make penances for the relationship, perceiving that the excursion of development and investigation is improved by the presence of a strong and cherishing accomplice.

Besides, praise the excursion of development and change inside your connections, perceiving that individual and aggregate advancement is a continuous interaction. Embrace the promising and less promising times, the victories and difficulties, as any open doors for picking up, recuperating, and development. By encouraging a culture of development and shared encounters, you make a dynamic and lively relationship that proceeds to develop and thrive over the long run.

At last, putting resources into development and shared encounters inside your connections isn't just about making recollections; it is tied in with extending closeness, cultivating association, and advancing the texture of your coexistences. Thus, try to put resources into one another's development and prosperity, and try to set out on new undertakings and encounters together, for inside the hug of shared encounters lies the genuine enchantment and magnificence of significant associations.

6

Chapter 6: Embracing Change and Adaptability

Grasping the Idea of Progress

In the great embroidery of life, change arises as the steady string that winds around its way through the texture of our reality. It is a consistently present power, molding our encounters, forming our personalities, and molding our general surroundings. To genuinely embrace change is to initially grasp its tendency - to remember it not as an interruption to business as usual, but rather as a basic piece of the human excursion.

Start by recognizing the certainty of progress as a major part of the human experience. Consider previous encounters of progress, both of all shapes and sizes, and the examples gained from exploring changes. Consider how each change in conditions has pushed you forward on your excursion, opening new entryways, and offering new points of view. By embracing change as a characteristic and unavoidable piece of life, you lay the foundation for embracing its extraordinary power.

Also, mull over the smoothness and temporariness of life, perceiving that change is the actual substance of presence. Similarly as the seasons change from spring to summer to fall, so too do our lives go through patterns of development, change, and recharging. Embrace change as an impetus for development and advancement, welcoming it to shape and shape you into the individual you are intended to turn into.

As you develop how you might interpret the idea of progress, develop a feeling of acknowledgment and give up. Discharge the need to stick to the natural and the agreeable, and on second thought, embrace the back and forth movement of existence with effortlessness and composure. By relinquishing opposition and embracing change with an open heart and brain, you make space for additional opportunities to unfurl and for change to flourish.

Eventually, understanding the idea of progress isn't just about scholarly appreciation; it is tied in with embracing change as an inborn and fundamental part of the human experience. By perceiving its certainty, smoothness, and extraordinary power, you enable yourself to explore life's changes with fortitude, strength, and beauty. In this way, try to embrace change as the dependable friend on your excursion, realizing that inside its hug lies the potential for development, revelation, and significant change.

Developing Flexibility

In the steadily changing scene of life, flexibility arises as a crucial expertise, empowering us to explore the exciting bends in the road of our excursion with strength and effortlessness. To develop flexibility is to embrace change as a chance for development and change, as opposed to a danger to be dreaded or stood up to.

Start by fostering an outlook of versatility, perceiving that change isn't something to be kept away from or dreaded, but instead an innate piece of the human experience. Embrace the possibility that adaptability and versatility are critical to flourishing in a consistently impacting world. Develop a feeling of interest and receptiveness to new encounters, permitting yourself to embrace the obscure with mental fortitude and excitement.

Practice adaptability notwithstanding vulnerability, adjusting to new conditions with beauty and fortitude. Perceive that life seldom unfurls as indicated by our arrangements, and that the capacity to turn and change course when fundamental is fundamental for exploring life's difficulties. Develop an eagerness to relinquish unbending assumptions and embrace the open doors that change brings, in any event, when they might be unforeseen or awkward.

Also, develop strength despite difficulty, perceiving that mishaps and hindrances are inescapable pieces of the excursion. As opposed to review them as unconquerable obstructions, consider them to be potential open doors for development and learning. Draw upon your internal stores of solidarity and assurance, taking advantage of the force of positive reasoning and self-conviction to defeat hindrances with effortlessness and versatility.

As you develop versatility, be aware of the significance of taking care of oneself and self-empathy. Exploring change can be genuinely and intellectually burdening, so it's fundamental to focus on your prosperity and support yourself through times of progress. Practice care, contemplation, and other taking care of oneself strategies to develop internal harmony and flexibility, permitting yourself to explore change with clearness and levelheadedness.

Eventually, developing flexibility isn't just about enduring change; it's tied in with flourishing despite vulnerability and embracing the amazing open doors for development and change that it brings. By fostering an outlook of versatility, rehearsing adaptability and flexibility, and focusing on taking care of oneself, you enable yourself to explore life's changes with fortitude, elegance, and strength. Thus, try to develop flexibility as a core value on your excursion, realizing that inside its hug lies the ability to explore change with elegance and strength.

Embracing Vulnerability

In the perplexing embroidery of life, vulnerability arises as a steady friend, winding around its way through the texture of our reality with flighty exciting bends in the road. However, instead of review vulnerability as a wellspring of dread or uneasiness, we can decide to embrace it with interest and receptiveness, perceiving that inside the obscure untruths the potential for development, revelation, and change.

Embrace the obscure with a feeling of interest and miracle, perceiving that vulnerability is a characteristic piece of the human experience. Instead of opposing or staying away from vulnerability, incline toward it with an open heart and brain, permitting yourself to investigate additional opportunities and embrace the potential open doors that emerge. Develop a feeling of versatility and trust in your capacity to explore vulnerability, confiding in your internal strength and instinct to direct you through life's exciting bends in the road.

Besides, perceive that vulnerability frequently fills in as an impetus for development and development, pushing us out of our usual ranges of familiarity and moving us to grow our viewpoints. Embrace vulnerability as an encouragement to step into the obscure, to investigate new ways and conceivable outcomes, and to extend past the impediments of our usual range of familiarity. By embracing vulnerability with boldness and assurance, we set out open doors for individual and otherworldly development that can prompt significant change.

As you explore vulnerability, develop a feeling of strength and flexibility, realizing that you have the inward assets and capacities to face life's hardships with elegance and fortitude. Practice care and self-empathy as apparatuses for exploring vulnerability, permitting yourself to remain grounded and focused in the midst of the disorder of progress. Rest on your encouraging group of people of companions, family, and friends and family for direction and support, realizing that you are in good company on this excursion.

Moreover, perceive that vulnerability isn't something to be dreaded, yet rather a characteristic and unavoidable piece of the human experience. Embrace vulnerability as an educator, offering examples in strength, boldness, and self-revelation. By embracing vulnerability with an open heart and brain, you enable yourself to explore life's difficulties with effortlessness and versatility, knowing that inside the obscure untruths the potential for development, change, and significant understanding.

Eventually, embracing vulnerability isn't just about exploring life's difficulties; it's tied in with embracing the extravagance and intricacy of the human experience. By inclining toward vulnerability with boldness and interest, we free ourselves up to additional opportunities and valuable open doors for development and self-revelation. Thus, try to embrace vulnerability as a core value on your excursion, realizing that inside its hug lies the potential for significant change and self-awareness.

Embracing Change as an Impetus for Development

Change, with its always moving tides, frequently shows up excluded, disturbing the cadence of our lives and testing the recognizable scenes of our reality. However, concealed inside the folds of progress lies a strong impetus for development and change, welcoming us to advance, adjust, and grow past the limits of our usual range of familiarity.

Shift your viewpoint on change, seeing it not as a danger to be dreaded or opposed, yet as an entryway to additional opportunities and potential open doors. Embrace change as a characteristic and inescapable piece of life's excursion, perceiving that it offers ripe ground for individual and otherworldly development. By reexamining change as an impetus for development, you enable yourself to explore life's changes with boldness, strength, and an open heart.

Embrace change as a potential chance to get out of your usual range of familiarity and investigate new skylines. Perceive that development frequently happens beyond the natural limits of routine and consistency, where the seeds of change can flourish and thrive. Embrace change as a call to experience, welcoming you to leave on an excursion of self-disclosure, investigation, and development.

Besides, view change as a challenge to deliver what no longer serves you and embrace additional opportunities that line up with your bona fide self. Relinquish obsolete convictions, examples, and connections that keep you fastened to the past, and welcome in the new energies of recharging and resurrection. Embrace change as a chance to reevaluate yourself, to investigate new interests and pursuits, and to step into the completion of your true capacity.

As you explore change, develop a feeling of versatility and flexibility, realizing that you have the inward assets and capacities to endure life's hardships with elegance and boldness. Practice care and self-empathy as instruments for exploring change, permitting yourself to remain grounded and focused in the midst of the vulnerability of change. Rest on your encouraging group of people of companions, family, and friends and family for direction and consolation, realizing that you are in good company on this excursion.

Besides, perceive that change is certainly not a direct interaction yet a dynamic and consistently developing excursion of development and self-revelation. Embrace the exciting bends in the road, the promising and less promising times, as any open doors for getting the hang of, recuperating, and change. By embracing change as an impetus for development, you free yourself up to additional opportunities and open doors for extension and advancement.

Eventually, embracing change as an impetus for development isn't just about enduring life's advances; it's tied in with flourishing in the midst of the unavoidable trends, realizing that inside their hug lies the potential for significant change and self-improvement. Thus, try to embrace change as a core value on your excursion, realizing that inside its hug lies the ability to open your actual potential and carry on with an existence of significant importance.

Building Strength Notwithstanding Change

In the flighty excursion of life, change frequently introduces itself as an imposing power, testing our feeling of steadiness and security. However, inside the pot of progress lies the chance to develop versatility - the internal strength and guts to endure life's hardships with elegance and mental fortitude.

Foster procedures for building flexibility despite change, perceiving that versatility isn't just about returning from difficulty yet about flourishing in the midst of vulnerability and commotion. Develop a mentality of versatility, seeing difficulties as any open doors for development and advancing instead of unfavorable obstructions. Embrace the conviction that you have the inward assets and abilities to explore change with fortitude and strength.

Practice care as a device for building strength, permitting yourself to remain present and grounded in the midst of the choppiness of progress. Develop a feeling of inward quiet and composure, realizing that you have the strength and flexibility to face life's hardships with elegance and fortitude. By developing care, you make space for self-reflection and mindfulness, permitting you to explore change with lucidity and poise.

Put resources into taking care of oneself for the purpose of sustaining strength notwithstanding change. Focus on exercises that support your body, psyche, and soul, like activity, reflection, and investing energy in nature. Take part in rehearses that advance profound prosperity, for example, journaling, imaginative articulation, and associating with friends and family. By focusing on taking care of oneself, you recharge your internal stores of solidarity and versatility, permitting you to explore change with elegance and strength.

Look for help from your encouraging group of people of companions, family, and friends and family as you explore change. Rest on others for direction, consolation, and basic reassurance, realizing that you are in good company on this excursion. By encircling yourself with a strong local area, you make an organization of assets and associations that can assist you with exploring change no sweat and versatility.

Besides, develop an identity sympathy and self-acknowledgment as you explore change. Be delicate with yourself during seasons of change, recognizing the difficulties and hardships that might emerge, and offering yourself graciousness and understanding. By rehearsing self-empathy, you fabricate versatility from the inside, encouraging a feeling of inward strength and certainty that can help you through even extremely testing times.

Eventually, building flexibility despite change isn't just about enduring life's advances; it's tied in with flourishing in the midst of vulnerability and commotion, realizing that you have the internal assets and abilities to explore change with effortlessness and mental fortitude. In this way, try to develop flexibility as a core value on your excursion, realizing that inside its hug lies the ability to explore change with strength, boldness, and elegance.

7

Chapter 7: Practicing Gratitude and Mindfulness

Figuring out the Force of Appreciation

In the embroidery of human experience, appreciation arises as a strong string that winds around its way through the texture of our lives, enhancing our connections, encouraging versatility, and saturating every second with a significant feeling of importance and reason. To really comprehend the force of appreciation is to perceive its groundbreaking impacts on our psychological, profound, and actual prosperity, and to embrace it as a core value in our day to day routines.

Start by investigating the horde manners by which appreciation can emphatically affect your life. Ponder minutes when you have encountered certified appreciation - maybe for the love of a companion, the magnificence of nature, or the straightforward delights of regular day to day existence. Notice how these snapshots of appreciation have brought a feeling of warmth, satisfaction, and association, hoisting your temperament and moving your viewpoint on life's difficulties.

Also, dig into the logical exploration that highlights the significant advantages of appreciation on our wellbeing and prosperity. Studies have shown that developing an outlook of appreciation can prompt more noteworthy joy, further developed connections, and improved in general life fulfillment. Appreciation has been connected to decreased degrees of stress and uneasiness, worked on safe capability, and, surprisingly, better rest quality. By understanding the science behind appreciation, you can acquire a more profound appreciation for its extraordinary power and the significant effect it can have on your life.

As you extend how you might interpret the force of appreciation, develop an everyday appreciation practice to saddle its advantages in your own life. This training can take many structures, from keeping an appreciation diary to offering thanks out loud to friends and family or just pausing for a minute every day to consider the gifts in your day to day existence. By making appreciation a customary piece of your daily schedule, you train your brain to zero in on the positive parts of life, even notwithstanding difficulties and difficulty.

Moreover, perceive that appreciation isn't just a transient inclination or feeling, yet an approach to being - a central direction toward life that colors each part of our reality. Develop a mentality of appreciation in your connections with others, communicating appreciation for their thoughtfulness, backing, and presence in your life. Notice the little endowments that encompass you every day - the glow of the sun all over, the giggling of kids playing, the excellence of a sprouting bloom - and permit yourself to be loaded up with appreciation for the wealth of life's encounters.

Eventually, understanding the influence of appreciation isn't just about perceiving its advantages; it's tied in with embracing it as a core value in your regular routine, developing an outlook of appreciation and overflow that changes your connections, upgrades your prosperity, and enhances your experience of life. In this way, set out to embrace the force of appreciation, realizing that inside its hug lies the way to opening an existence of satisfaction, satisfaction, and importance.

Developing an Appreciation Practice

Setting out on an excursion of appreciation starts with the cognizant choice to develop an appreciation practice - a conscious and deliberate work to develop appreciation and gratefulness for the favors, of all shapes and sizes, that improve our lives. This training fills in as a useful asset for moving our viewpoint, encouraging a feeling of overflow, and supporting a profound feeling of happiness and satisfaction.

To develop an appreciation practice, begin via cutting out time every day to consider the things you are thankful for. This can appear as a day to day appreciation diary, where you record three to five things you are grateful for every day. These can be basic joys, like a warm cup of tea, a wonderful dawn, or a nice thought from a companion, or bigger endowments, like the affection for family, great wellbeing, or a satisfying profession. By deliberately recognizing the endowments in your day to day existence, you train your brain to zero in on the positive parts of life, as opposed to harping on where is missing or going wrong.

As well as keeping an appreciation diary, consider integrating appreciation rehearses into your everyday daily schedule. Begin every day with an appreciation contemplation or petition, communicating gratitude for the gifts in your day to day existence and establishing an uplifting vibe for the day ahead. Over the course of the day, delay to see and value the magnificence and overflow that encompasses you - the glow of the sun all over, the sound of birdsong in the air, the grin of a more bizarre cruising by. By developing an outlook of appreciation in your regular routine, you make space for satisfaction, appreciation, and marvel to prosper.

Besides, develop a demeanor of appreciation in your connections with others. Get some margin to communicate appreciation for the graciousness, backing, and love that others show you, whether through a sincere card to say thanks, a warm embrace, or a straightforward expression of much obliged. By recognizing the commitments of others and offering thanks for their presence in your life, you develop your associations and encourage a feeling of warmth and having a place.

As you develop an appreciation practice, show restraint toward yourself and permit space for flaw. Every so often, it could be simpler to feel appreciative than others, and that is fine. The key is to move toward your appreciation practice with an open heart and a readiness to embrace the overflow that encompasses you, even amidst life's difficulties and battles.

At last, developing an appreciation practice isn't just about remembering your good fortune; it's tied in with developing a mentality of appreciation and overflow that pervades each part of your life. By embracing appreciation as an approach to being, you free yourself up to a more profound feeling of euphoria, satisfaction, and association with your general surroundings. Thus, set out to develop an appreciation work on, realizing that inside its hug lies the way to opening an existence of overflow and bliss.

Embracing Care

In the speedy rushing about of current life, moving cleared away by the flows of hecticness, moving away from the current second and the extravagance of our lived experience is simple. However, in the midst of the disorder of our day to day routines, there exists a strong remedy - care. Established in the old act of contemplation and present-second mindfulness, care offers us an entryway into the present time and place, welcoming us to stir to the completion of every second with transparency, interest, and acknowledgment.

At its center, care is the act of carrying our consideration and attention to the current second, without judgment or connection. It includes tuning into our viewpoints, feelings, and sensations with a feeling of interest and non-reactivity, permitting us to develop a more profound comprehension of ourselves and our general surroundings. By securing ourselves right now, we free ourselves from the hold of remorseful thoughts and future nerves, tracking down shelter in the present time and place.

To embrace care in your everyday existence, start by investigating basic care rehearses that you can integrate into your daily practice. This could be essentially as direct as taking a couple of seconds every day to zero in on your breath, seeing the ascent and fall of your chest and the vibe of air going through your noses. On the other hand, you could rehearse careful eating, relishing each nibble of food with mindfulness and appreciation for the sustenance it gives. Anything structure your care practice takes, move toward it with an open heart and a feeling of interest, permitting yourself to be completely present in every second.

Besides, investigate the idea of care as an approach to being - a major direction toward life that saturates each part of our reality. Develop care in your collaborations with others, listening profoundly and mindfully to their words, and answering with consideration and empathy. Carry care to your everyday exercises, whether it's washing dishes, strolling in nature, or essentially sitting unobtrusively and noticing your general surroundings. By implanting your existence with care, you set out open doors for more profound association, presence, and happiness.

As you extend your act of care, be delicate with yourself and permit space for flaw. Care isn't tied in with accomplishing a condition of wonderful mindfulness or edification however about developing a feeling of receptiveness and acknowledgment toward whatever emerges right now. Notice when your psyche meanders or when you become derailed in thought, presence tenderly aide your consideration back to the current second with graciousness and sympathy.

At last, embracing care isn't just about developing an act of present-second mindfulness; it's tied in with developing an approach to being that brings more prominent clearness, harmony, and association with our lives. By embracing care as a core value in our regular routines, we free ourselves up to the magnificence and lavishness of every second, tracking down bliss and satisfaction in the present time and place. Thus, set out to embrace care as a pathway to more prominent presence, mindfulness, and aliveness, realizing that inside its hug lies the way to opening an existence of significant importance and satisfaction.

Living with Goal and Mindfulness

At the core of care lies the act of living with goal and mindfulness - the cognizant decision to carry our complete focus and presence to every second, to draw in with existence with reason and clearness. Living with aim implies adjusting our considerations, words, and activities with our most profound qualities and desires, while living with mindfulness includes developing a profound feeling of presence and aliveness in every second.

To embrace living with expectation and mindfulness, begin by explaining your qualities and needs throughout everyday life. Ponder the main thing to you - your connections, your interests, your feeling of direction - and recognize the activities and ways of behaving that line up with these qualities. By living in arrangement with your qualities, you make a feeling of consistency and legitimacy that carries more prominent importance and satisfaction to your life.

Besides, develop a feeling of care in your everyday exercises, carrying your complete focus and presence to every second. Whether you're washing dishes, strolling in nature, or having a discussion with a friend or family member, work on being completely present and drawn in with anything that you're doing. Notice the sensations, considerations, and feelings that emerge in every second, without judgment or connection, and permit yourself to encounter existence with a feeling of interest and marvel.

As you develop living with aim and mindfulness, focus on the effect of your viewpoints, words, and activities on yourself as well as other people. Notice how your expectations shape your experience of life and the nature of your connections. Develop a feeling of graciousness and empathy toward yourself as well as other people, perceiving that we are defective creatures doing all that can be expected in every second.

Besides, work on carrying care and purposefulness to testing circumstances and troublesome feelings. Rather than responding hastily or consequently, respite and take a couple of full breaths, permitting yourself to answer with clearness and sympathy. By bringing a feeling of care and goal to troublesome minutes, you make space for grasping, mending, and development.

At last, living with expectation and mindfulness isn't just about being available in every second; it's tied in with living in arrangement with our most profound qualities and yearnings, and drawing in with existence with reason and lucidity. By embracing care and deliberateness as core values in our day to day routines, we free ourselves up to a more profound feeling of importance, satisfaction, and association with our general surroundings. Thus, set out to live with aim and mindfulness, realizing that inside its hug lies the way to opening an existence of significant reason and satisfaction.

Discovering a sense of reconciliation and Satisfaction

Amidst life's hurrying around, in the midst of the consistently changing tides of presence, lies the significant chance to discover a genuine sense of reconciliation and happiness - not in that frame of mind of outer accomplishments or material belongings, however in the tranquil snapshots of presence, association, and appreciation. To discover a sense of harmony and satisfaction is to develop a profound feeling of internal prosperity that rises above the changes of life's conditions, securing us in a position of serenity and poise.

Start by embracing the current second as the doorway to harmony and happiness. Rather than becoming involved with second thoughts of the past or tensions about the future, work on establishing yourself in the present time and place. Develop a feeling of presence and aliveness in every second, permitting yourself to completely draw in with anything that you're doing - whether it's tasting some tea, going for a stroll in nature, or investing energy with friends and family. By carrying your complete focus and attention to the current second, you set out open doors for euphoria, association, and satisfaction to thrive.

Besides, develop a feeling of appreciation for the favors that have large amounts of your life. Take time every day to think about the things you are grateful for - the adoration for loved ones, the excellence of nature, the straightforward delights of regular daily existence. By developing a demeanor of appreciation, you shift your concentration based on the thing is missing to what is plentiful, encouraging a profound feeling of happiness and appreciation for the extravagance of life's encounters.

As you develop harmony and satisfaction, work on relinquishing connections and assumptions that keep you fastened to sensations of discontent and distress. Perceive that genuine harmony emerges not from outside conditions but rather from the inside, from a position of acknowledgment and give up to what is. Relinquish the need to control or control life's results, and on second thought, trust in the innate insight of the universe to unfurl as it will.

Moreover, practice taking care of oneself for of sustaining harmony and happiness inside yourself. Focus on exercises that feed your body, psyche, and soul, whether it's activity, contemplation, imaginative articulation, or investing energy in nature. By focusing on taking care of oneself, you renew your inward holds of energy and imperativeness, permitting you to explore life's difficulties no sweat and poise.

At last, discovering a genuine sense of reconciliation and satisfaction isn't just about looking for outside wellsprings of joy or satisfaction; it's tied in with developing a profound feeling of inward prosperity that rises above the changes of life's conditions. By embracing the current second, developing appreciation, relinquishing connections, and focusing on taking care of oneself, you set out open doors for harmony and happiness to thrive inside yourself. Thus, try to discover a lasting sense of reconciliation and satisfaction inside yourself, realizing that inside its hug lies the way to opening an existence of significant bliss, satisfaction, and importance.

8

Chapter 8: Serving Others and Making a Difference

Grasping the Force of Administration

Administration, in its substance, exemplifies a significant demonstration of magnanimity and empathy, rising above the limits of uniqueness to make waves of positive change that resonate all through the world. At its center, administration isn't just about performing beneficent deeds or offering help to those out of luck; it is tied in with perceiving the innate interconnectedness of all creatures and embracing the chance to have a significant effect on the existences of others and the world overall.

Start by digging into the extraordinary impacts of administration on private prosperity and satisfaction. As we stretch out ourselves in support of others, we offer help and backing as well as experience a profound feeling of association, reason, and satisfaction. Through thoughtful gestures, liberality, and empathy, we tap into the wellspring of human potential, touching off a feeling of bliss and satisfaction that rises above the limits of oneself.

Besides, consider the natural benefit of having a constructive outcome on the existences of others. Administration offers us the potential chance to step beyond ourselves, to rise above the limits of self image and personal circumstance, and to interface with the common humankind that ties us generally together. In serving others, we perceive that our singular prosperity is complicatedly connected to the prosperity of others, and that by elevating and supporting people around us, we add to the long term benefit of mankind.

As you extend how you might interpret the force of administration, think about the horde manners by which you can add to the prosperity of others. Administration takes many structures - from chipping in at a neighborhood sanctuary to listening carefully to a companion out of luck, from pushing for civil rights to spreading graciousness and empathy in your day to day collaborations. By embracing a feeling of administration, you free yourself up to a universe of opportunities for having a constructive outcome and cultivating a feeling of local area and association.

Besides, perceive that help isn't simply a one-time act yet a lifestyle - a consistent act of liberality, empathy, and benevolence that pervades each part of our reality. Whether through little thoughtful gestures or bigger endeavors to address fundamental treacheries, each demonstration of administration has the ability to make waves of positive change that stretch out a long ways past its nearby effect.

At last, understanding the force of administration isn't just about perceiving its advantages for other people; it's tied in with perceiving the significant effect it has on our own lives. By embracing a feeling of administration, we free ourselves up to a universe of importance, reason, and satisfaction, realizing that inside the demonstration of providing lies with the genuine pith of being human. In this way, set out to comprehend the force of administration, realizing that inside its hug lies the way to opening an existence of significant importance and satisfaction.

Developing a Feeling of Liberality

At the core of administration lies a feeling of liberality - a firmly established eagerness to give of oneself, without assumption for remuneration or acknowledgment, essentially to improve others and the world. Developing a feeling of liberality requires a basic change in context, from an outlook of shortage and personal circumstance to one of overflow and sympathy, perceiving the interconnectedness of all creatures and the inborn benefit of rewarding our networks.

Start by supporting an outlook of overflow, perceiving the abundance of assets, gifts, and favors that you have and the boundless potential for giving and sharing that exists inside you. Rather than review the world from the perspective of shortage - where assets are limited and contest is furious - embrace a mentality of overflow, where there is all that could possibly be needed to go around and potential open doors for liberality proliferate. By moving your point of view from shortage to overflow, you free yourself up to a universe of opportunities for offering in return and having a constructive outcome.

Besides, practice thoughtful gestures and administration for the purpose of communicating liberality and sympathy toward others. Whether it's chipping in your time and abilities to help a noble motivation, offering some assistance to a neighbor out of luck, or essentially broadening a benevolent word or signal to light up somebody's day, each demonstration of liberality has the ability to make a gradually expanding influence of positive change that stretches out a long ways past its nearby effect. By developing a feeling of liberality in your everyday existence, you elevate and uphold people around you as well as encourage a feeling of local area, association, and having a place.

As you develop your act of liberality, perceive the interconnectedness of all creatures and the significant effect that your activities have on your general surroundings. Each thoughtful gesture, regardless of how little, can possibly make a far reaching influence of positive change that resounds all through the world. By embracing a feeling of liberality, you become an impetus for change, moving others to show proactive kindness and make an existence where graciousness, empathy, and liberality are the standard as opposed to the special case.

Moreover, consider the natural delight and satisfaction that comes from giving of oneself and having a constructive outcome on the existences of others. As you develop a feeling of liberality, you tap into the wellspring of human potential, encountering a profound feeling of association, reason, and satisfaction that rises above the limits of oneself. By embracing liberality as a lifestyle, you set out open doors for satisfaction, importance, and satisfaction to thrive, both inside yourself and in your general surroundings.

Eventually, developing a feeling of liberality isn't just about rewarding others; it's tied in with perceiving the significant interconnectedness of all creatures and the innate benefit of adding to everyone's benefit. By embracing liberality as a core value in your life, you free yourself up to a universe of overflow, association, and probability, realizing that inside the demonstration of providing lies with the genuine quintessence of being human. Thus, try to develop a feeling of liberality, realizing that inside its hug lies the way to opening an existence of significant happiness, satisfaction, and reason.

Distinguishing Open doors for Administration

In the embroidery of life, open doors for administration proliferate - from loaning some assistance to those deprived to upholding for civil rights and foundational change. Distinguishing these potential open doors requires an eagerness to look past oneself, to perceive the necessities and difficulties confronting our networks, and to use our novel gifts, gifts, and assets to have a beneficial outcome.

Start by considering your own assets, interests, and subject matters. Consider how these interesting characteristics can be tackled to serve others and address squeezing social issues. Whether you have abilities in administration, correspondence, association, or imagination, there are endless ways of involving your gifts for everyone's benefit. By recognizing your solid areas, you can adjust your administration endeavors to your interests and interests, augmenting your effect and satisfaction simultaneously.

In addition, investigate various roads for administration inside your local area and then some. Volunteer your significant investment to help nearby associations and drives that line up with your qualities and needs. Whether it's serving dinners at a destitute haven, coaching understudies out of luck, or partaking in natural tidy up endeavors, there are heap valuable chances to have a beneficial outcome near and dear. Furthermore, think about taking part in support and activism to resolve fundamental issues and advance positive change for a bigger scope. By intensifying your voice and utilizing your impact, you can add to significant advancement on issues like civil rights, ecological supportability, and common freedoms.

As you distinguish open doors for administration, be available to investigating new roads and venturing beyond your usual range of familiarity. Embrace the obscure with a feeling of interest and experience, realizing that each new experience brings valuable open doors for development and learning. Whether it's chipping in locally, teaming up with new associations, or handling complex social issues, stretch yourself and grow your viewpoints in support of others.

Moreover, perceive that assistance isn't restricted to formal chipping in or magnanimous demonstrations; it can likewise appear as regular thoughtful gestures and empathy. Search for valuable chances to serve others in your day to day existence, whether it's contribution a listening ear to a companion out of luck, helping an outsider in trouble, or just spreading energy and generosity any place you go. By developing a feeling of administration in your everyday collaborations, you set out open doors for association, compassion, and generosity to prosper, improving both your life and the existences of people around you.

Eventually, distinguishing potential open doors for administration isn't just about rewarding others; it's tied in with perceiving the interconnectedness of all creatures and the inborn benefit of adding to everyone's benefit. By embracing a feeling of administration and utilizing your novel gifts and abilities to have a constructive outcome, you become an impetus for change, moving others to go along with you in making an existence where sympathy, compassion, and liberality are the core values of human connection. Thus, try to recognize potential open doors for administration, realizing that inside their hug lies the way to opening an existence of significant reason, satisfaction, and importance.

Having a Significant Effect

Administration isn't just about performing demonstrations of good cause or offering help; it is tied in with making a significant and enduring effect on the existences of others and the world at large. To have a significant effect requires purposefulness, vision, and a guarantee to making positive change on the planet. It includes defining clear objectives and targets for your administration endeavors, distinguishing regions where you can have the best effect, and making an essential move to order certain change.

Start by setting expectations for your administration endeavors, explaining the objectives and goals you desire to accomplish. Whether it's resolving a particular social issue, supporting a minimized local area, or advancing natural supportability, get some margin to verbalize your vision for the effect you need to make. By setting clear expectations, you make a guide for your administration endeavors and guarantee that your activities are lined up with your qualities and needs.

In addition, make an essential move to rejuvenate your vision, utilizing your abilities, assets, and organizations to sanction positive change. Whether it's getting sorted out a raising money occasion, preparing local area individuals to help a reason, or pushing for strategy change, be proactive in chasing after your objectives and targets. Go ahead with reasonable plans of action, adjust and enhance, and endure notwithstanding difficulties and misfortunes. By making an essential move, you expand your effect and viability as a change-creator on the planet.

As you work to have a significant effect, perceive the significance of coordinated effort and organization in accomplishing your objectives. Search out chances to team up with similar people and associations who share your vision and values. By pooling your assets and aptitude, you can enhance your effect and reach, making collaborations that lead to more prominent aggregate activity and positive change. Moreover, be available to gaining from others and integrating assorted viewpoints and thoughts into your methodology. By embracing cooperation and association, you set out open doors for advancement, imagination, and common help in your administration endeavors.

Moreover, measure and assess your effect on target progress toward your objectives and goals. Carve out opportunity to consider the results of your administration endeavors, both quantitative and subjective, and survey the adequacy of your methodology. Celebrate victories, gain from disappointments, and use criticism to refine and further develop your procedures pushing ahead. By taking on a mentality of ceaseless learning and improvement, you guarantee that your administration endeavors are significant, manageable, and lined up with your vision for positive change.

Eventually, having a significant effect isn't just about the moves you make; it's about the enduring heritage you abandon and the positive change you make on the planet. By setting clear goals, making an essential move, teaming up with others, and estimating your effect, you can have a significant effect in the existences of others and add to the general benefit of humankind. In this way, set out to have a significant effect, realizing that inside your endeavors lies the ability to make an existence where empathy, equity, and equity win.

Sustaining the Gradually expanding influence of Administration

As you set out on your excursion of administration and have a constructive outcome in the existences of others, perceive the intrinsic force of your activities to make a far reaching influence of positive change that stretches out a long ways past their nearby effect. Administration has an approach to rising above limits and rousing others to participate in the aggregate work to make a superior world. By sustaining the expanding influence of administration, you amplify your effect as well as make a tradition of sympathy, graciousness, and liberality that resounds all through the world.

Most importantly, perceive that each demonstration of administration, regardless of how little, can possibly rouse others and make a far reaching influence of positive change. Whether it's chipping in at a neighborhood cover, sorting out a local area cleanup, or supporting for civil rights, your activities send a strong message to others that positive change is conceivable and that every individual has the ability to have an effect. By showing others how its done and exhibiting the effect of administration in your own life, you move others to follow after accordingly and go along with you in the work to make an additional empathetic and simply world.

Besides, celebrate and intensify the effect of your administration endeavors by imparting your encounters and stories to other people. Utilize your voice and stage to bring issues to light about the issues you care about and move others to reach out. Whether through web-based entertainment, local area occasions, or narrating, share the tales of those you have helped and the positive effect your administration has had on their lives. By focusing a light on the gradually expanding influence of administration, you move others to participate in the aggregate work to make positive change and have a significant effect on the planet.

Also, set out open doors for others to reach out and add to the work to make positive change. Whether it's getting sorted out volunteer occasions, raising support missions, or backing drives, welcome others to go along with you in the excursion of administration and have an unmistakable effect in their networks and then some. By encouraging a feeling of local area and cooperation, you make a far reaching influence of administration that stretches out a long ways past your singular endeavors, preparing an aggregate power for good that has the ability to make groundbreaking change on the planet.

Besides, perceive and recognize the gradually expanding influence of administration in your own life and the significant effect it has on your prosperity and feeling of satisfaction. As you witness the positive change you can make through your administration endeavors, permit yourself to be loaded up with a feeling of appreciation and appreciation for the chance to have an effect in the existences of others. By sustaining the expanding influence of administration in your own life, you develop a profound feeling of direction, importance, and satisfaction that enhances each part of your reality.

Eventually, supporting the expanding influence of administration isn't just about amplifying your effect or moving others to reach out; it's tied in with making a tradition of sympathy, thoughtfulness, and liberality that rises above the limits of reality. By embracing the gradually expanding influence of administration, you become an impetus for positive change on the planet, motivating others to go along with you in the work to make an all the more, humane, and fair world for all. In this way, set out to sustain the expanding influence of administration, realizing that inside its hug lies the ability to make an existence where love, sympathy, and benevolence rule.

Chapter 9: Living with Intentionality

Grasping Purposefulness

Living with deliberateness is something beyond floating through life; it's about effectively captivating with every second, choice, and activity with reason and mindfulness. At its center, deliberateness is an intentional and cognizant way to deal with life, where each decision is made with lucidity, arrangement with individual qualities, and a profound feeling of direction. By understanding the influence of deliberateness, we open the capacity to shape our encounters, diagram our own course, and develop a daily existence that is rich with significance and satisfaction.

Start by investigating the idea of deliberateness and its importance in significantly shaping our lives. Deliberateness welcomes us to move past autopilot and become dynamic members in our own reality. Rather than permitting conditions to direct our way, we make responsibility for decisions and moves, perceiving that every choice we make can possibly shape our present and future reality. By embracing deliberateness, we recover organization over our daily routines and enable ourselves to experience with more prominent reason and satisfaction.

In addition, perceive the significant effect that deliberateness can have on our general prosperity. At the point when we live with deliberateness, we approach existence with a reasonable internal compass and reason, prompting more prominent fulfillment, satisfaction, and joy. By adjusting our activities to our qualities and desires, we make a feeling of harmoniousness and genuineness that encourages internal harmony and congruity. Fundamentally, purposefulness fills in as a directing light, enlightening the way toward a day to day existence that is profoundly significant and satisfying.

As you dive further into the idea of purposefulness, consider how it appears in your own life. Consider the regions where you feel generally lined up with your qualities and reason, as well as those where you might be floating off kilter. Check out your objectives, desires, and needs, and consider how purposeful living can assist you with accomplishing them. By developing a more prominent familiarity with your own goals and inspirations, you can start to pursue more cognizant decisions that help your general prosperity and lead to an existence of more prominent satisfaction.

Eventually, understanding purposefulness isn't just about intellectualizing the idea; it's tied in with epitomizing it in each part of our lives. By embracing deliberateness as a core value, we enable ourselves to live with more prominent lucidity, reason, and genuineness, opening the potential for significant development and change. In this way, try to embrace deliberateness as a pathway to a daily existence that is profoundly lined up with your qualities and yearnings, realizing that inside its hug lies the way to opening an existence of genuine satisfaction and significance.

Developing Lucidity of Direction

Key to living with deliberateness is developing a profound feeling of lucidity in regards to our motivation throughout everyday life. This lucidity fills in as a directing light, enlightening the way ahead and giving an internal compass and concentration in the midst of life's intricacies and vulnerabilities. Developing lucidity of direction includes a course of self-reflection, thoughtfulness, and arrangement with our most profound qualities, interests, and goals.

Start by leaving on an excursion of self-revelation, investigating the center parts of your personality, values, and convictions. Ponder your interests, interests, and the exercises that give you the best pleasure and satisfaction. Consider the minutes in your day to day existence when you have felt generally invigorated, drew in, and lined up with your actual self. By diving into your internal scene, you can reveal signs about your motivation and the extraordinary gifts and abilities you bring to the table for the world.

Also, set aside some margin to verbalize your qualities and needs, distinguishing the standards and beliefs that are mean quite a bit to you. Consider what makes the biggest difference in your life - whether it's family, connections, self-improvement, or having an effect on the planet - and ponder how these qualities line up with your feeling of direction. By explaining your qualities, you make an establishment whereupon to construct a daily existence that is profoundly significant and satisfying.

As you develop lucidity of direction, put forth significant objectives and expectations that line up with your qualities and goals. Consider what you desire to accomplish in your own and proficient life, and how these objectives add to your feeling of direction and satisfaction. Stall your objectives into noteworthy stages and make a guide for accomplishing them, considering adaptability and transformation as you explore the excursion ahead.

Moreover, look for chances to adjust your everyday activities and choices to your feeling of direction and values. Consider how you can imbue purposefulness into your everyday schedules and propensities, pursuing decisions that help your general prosperity and add to your drawn out objectives. Whether it's rehearsing care, focusing on taking care of oneself, or participating in exercises that give you pleasure and satisfaction, develop propensities that support your feeling of direction and arrangement with your qualities.

Eventually, developing clearness of direction is a continuous excursion of self-revelation and arrangement with our most profound insights. By diving into our internal scene, explaining our qualities, and defining significant objectives, we make a guide for living with deliberateness and reason. Embrace the cycle with interest, transparency, and an eagerness to investigate additional opportunities, realizing that inside the profundities of self-revelation lies the way to opening an existence of genuine significance and satisfaction.

Embracing Careful Direction

Living with purposefulness includes embracing care in our dynamic cycles, permitting us to move toward decisions with more noteworthy mindfulness, lucidity, and arrangement with our qualities and needs. Careful dynamic welcomes us to stop, reflect, and consider the outcomes of our activities prior to pushing ahead, guaranteeing that our decisions are in accordance with our feeling of direction and in general prosperity.

Start by developing an act of care in your everyday existence, coordinating snapshots of presence and mindfulness into your schedules and exercises. Whether through reflection, profound breathing activities, or basically tuning into your faculties as you approach your day, develop a feeling of groundedness and presence that permits you to move toward decision-production with clearness and aim.

Besides, carry care to the dynamic interaction itself, carving out opportunity to consider the choices before you and the possible results of every decision. Consider how every choice lines up with your qualities, needs, and long haul objectives, and assess the possible advantages and disadvantages of each. By moving toward choices with care, you can settle on decisions that are established in astuteness, clearness, and arrangement with your feeling of direction.

As you embrace careful direction, be available to paying attention to your instinct and inward direction, confiding in your natural insight to direct you toward decisions that are in accordance with your most noteworthy great. Develop a feeling of interest and receptiveness as you investigate various choices and conceivable outcomes, permitting yourself to be directed by a profound feeling of knowing and arrangement with your qualities and goals.

Besides, practice acumen in your dynamic cycle, recognizing motivations driven by self image or outside tensions and decisions that are lined up with your actual longings and goals. Tune into your inward voice and instinct, and focus on any signs or signals that might emerge as you think about your choices. By developing insight, you can go with decisions that are real, adjusted, and steady of your general prosperity.

Eventually, embracing careful direction is tied in with developing a more profound feeling of mindfulness and presence in our decisions, permitting us to explore existence with more prominent clearness, reason, and arrangement with our qualities. By carrying care to our dynamic cycles, we enable ourselves to pursue decisions that honor our actual selves and add to a daily existence that is rich with importance and satisfaction. In this way, try to embrace careful decision-production as a pathway to living with deliberateness, realizing that inside its hug lies the way to opening an existence of genuine validness and reason.

Making Everyday Ceremonies and Propensities

A fundamental part of living with deliberateness includes the formation of day to day customs and propensities that help our excursion toward an existence of direction and satisfaction. These ceremonies act as anchors in the midst of the bedlam of day to day existence, giving us snapshots of establishing, reflection, and association with our most profound qualities and desires. By deliberately making our day to day schedules, we can develop a feeling of care, presence, and arrangement with our feeling of direction.

Start by distinguishing customs and propensities that impact you and backing your general prosperity and objectives. Consider exercises like contemplation, journaling, exercise, or appreciation practice - exercises that sustain your psyche, body, and soul and assist you with developing a more profound feeling of presence and mindfulness in your day to day existence. By integrating these practices into your day to day schedules, you set out open doors for self-reflection, development, and association with your deepest self.

Besides, lay out an everyday schedule that lines up with your qualities, needs, and objectives. Put away devoted time every day for exercises that are vital to you - whether it's chasing after a purposeful venture, investing quality energy with friends and family, or participating in taking care of oneself practices. By making construction and consistency in your day to day schedules, you make space for deliberate living and develop a feeling of direction and satisfaction in your regular day to day existence.

As you lay out your everyday customs and propensities, be aware of the effect they have on your general prosperity and feeling of arrangement with your qualities. Focus on how these practices cause you to feel - genuinely, intellectually, and inwardly - and change them on a case by case basis to all the more likely help your necessities and yearnings. By remaining receptive to your internal insight and instinct, you can tweak your day to day schedules to all the more likely work well for your generally speaking being and feeling of direction.

Besides, utilize your everyday customs and propensities as any open doors for self-reflection and development. Put away opportunity every day for reflection, journaling, or care work on, permitting yourself to interface with your deepest contemplations, sentiments, and goals. By making space for self-appearance in your everyday schedules, you cultivate a more profound identity mindfulness and arrangement with your qualities and objectives, engaging you to live with more noteworthy deliberateness and reason.

At last, making day to day ceremonies and propensities is about something beyond making a cursory effort; it's tied in with implanting significance, reason, and purposefulness into each part of our lives. By purposefully making our day to day schedules, we set out open doors for development, association, and arrangement with our most profound qualities and desires. In this way, try to make everyday customs and propensities that help your excursion toward an existence of direction and satisfaction, realizing that inside their hug lies the way to opening your fullest potential and most genuine self.

Exploring Difficulties with Strength

Living with deliberateness unavoidably includes experiencing difficulties and misfortunes en route. In any case, the manner in which we explore these snags can extraordinarily affect our capacity to remain consistent with our feeling of direction and forge ahead with our excursion of purposeful living. Creating flexibility - the capacity to return from difficulty with strength and effortlessness - is fundamental for keeping up with our obligation to living with purposefulness, even despite misfortune.

Start by rethinking difficulties as any open doors for development and learning. Rather than review mishaps as inconceivable deterrents, consider them to be solicitations to extend your versatility and reinforce your purpose. Embrace a development outlook, perceiving that each challenge offers important examples and experiences that can assist you with developing further and stronger over the long haul.

Besides, practice self-sympathy and consideration toward yourself during troublesome times. Indulge yourself with the very level of understanding and backing that you would propose to a dear companion confronting a comparative test. Recognize your feelings and permit yourself to feel them completely, without judgment or self-analysis. By rehearsing self-sympathy, you develop a feeling of internal strength and flexibility that permits you to face life's hardships no sweat and elegance.

As you explore difficulties, rest on your encouraging group of people for direction and consolation. Connect with companions, relatives, or coaches who can offer help, point of view, and intelligence during troublesome times. Permit yourself to be defenseless and request help when you want it, realizing that you don't need to confront difficulties alone. By encircling yourself with a steady local area, you make a security net of adoration and consolation that reinforces your strength and assists you with remaining consistent with your way of purposeful living.

Besides, practice appreciation and care as apparatuses for developing strength even with misfortune. Take time every day to ponder the things you are thankful for, even amidst difficulties. Develop a feeling of presence and mindfulness right now, zeroing in on what you have some control over and relinquishing what is outside of your reach. By developing appreciation and care, you encourage a feeling of internal harmony and versatility that engages you to explore life's difficulties with effortlessness and flexibility.

Eventually, exploring difficulties with strength is tied in with embracing the innate back and forth movement of existence with receptiveness, boldness, and elegance. By developing flexibility, rehearsing self-sympathy, resting on your encouraging group of people, and embracing appreciation and care, you can endure life's hardships with strength and versatility, remaining consistent with your way of purposeful living even notwithstanding affliction. In this way, set out to explore difficulties with flexibility, knowing that inside your capacity to return quickly lies the way to opening an existence of genuine satisfaction and reason.

I O

Chapter 10: Celebrating Your Journey

Thinking about Achievements and Accomplishments

As you arrive at the climax of your excursion toward purposeful living, it's vital for stop and consider the achievements and accomplishments that have denoted your way. Pause for a minute to recognize the headway you've made, the difficulties you've survived, and the development you've encountered en route. Commend the little triumphs - the snapshots of mental fortitude, flexibility, and assurance - that have moved you forward on your excursion toward an existence of direction and satisfaction.

Considering your achievements permits you to perceive the unmistakable proof of your advancement and development. Consider the objectives you've set for you and the means you've taken to accomplish them. Whether it's finishing an undertaking, arriving at an individual achievement, or conquering a critical test, every accomplishment is a demonstration of your devotion, determination, and obligation to living with purposefulness.

Besides, carve out opportunity to commend your accomplishments in a significant manner. Share your victories with friends and family, companions, or coaches who have upheld you en route. Permit yourself to loll in the delight and fulfillment of your achievements, realizing that they are an impression of your persistent effort, assurance, and flexibility.

Considering your achievements additionally gives an open door to appreciation and appreciation. Offer thanks for the encounters, open doors, and examples advanced en route. Perceive individuals who play had an impact in your excursion - the coaches who have directed you, the companions who have upheld you, and the friends and family who have supported you from the sidelines. By offering thanks for your excursion, you develop a feeling of overflow and satisfaction that enhances each part of your life.

At last, pondering your achievements and accomplishments is an approach to regarding your excursion and the headway you've made en route. It's a sign of how far you've come and a wellspring of motivation for the street ahead. In this way, pause for a minute to stop, reflect, and commend your accomplishments, realizing that inside their hug lies the way to opening an existence of genuine reason, satisfaction, and significance.

Offering Thanks for the Excursion

As you arrive at the last part of your excursion toward deliberate living, pause for a minute to develop a significant feeling of appreciation for the encounters, valuable open doors, and examples advanced en route. Appreciation is a strong practice that permits us to perceive the overflow and gifts in our lives, even in the midst of the difficulties and vulnerabilities. By offering thanks for the excursion, we honor the lavishness of our encounters and the development that has unfurled accordingly.

Start by considering the difficulties and mishaps you've experienced on your excursion and the examples they have instructed you. Consider the snapshots of battle and misfortune that have tried your flexibility and tirelessness, and recognize the strength and boldness it took to defeat them. By offering thanks for the difficulties, you embrace them as any open doors for development and change, perceiving the insight and strength they have conferred.

Additionally, offer thanks for the help and consolation of the people who have went with you on your excursion. Think about the companions, relatives, coaches, and partners who have given a shout out to you, offered direction and shrewdness, and gave a shoulder to rest on during troublesome times. Express sincere appreciation for their presence in your life and the manners by which they have added to your development and prosperity.

Moreover, offer thanks for the snapshots of delight, magnificence, and satisfaction that have improved your excursion. Ponder the encounters that have given you a feeling of pleasure, marvel, and stunningness - whether it's seeing an amazing nightfall, imparting chuckling to friends and family, or encountering snapshots of significant association and importance. By offering thanks for these minutes, you recognize the overflow and extravagance of life and develop a profound feeling of satisfaction and satisfaction.

As you offer thanks for the excursion, consider the manners by which it has molded you into the individual you are today. Consider the qualities, convictions, and yearnings that have arisen because of your encounters, and recognize the manners by which you have developed, advanced, and become more lined up with your actual self. By offering thanks for the excursion, you honor the groundbreaking force of purposeful living and perceive the significant effect it has had on your life.

Eventually, offering thanks for the excursion is an approach to recognizing the magnificence, extravagance, and intricacy of life. It's a suggestion to treasure every second, embrace each insight, and develop a feeling of appreciation for the actual excursion. In this way, pause for a minute to stop, reflect, and offer thanks for the excursion you've set out after, realizing that inside its hug lies the way to opening an existence of genuine satisfaction, reason, and importance.

Embracing Self-Sympathy and Acknowledgment

As you think about your excursion toward purposeful living, it's vital to embrace self-sympathy and acknowledgment for both yourself and the way you've voyaged. Living with deliberateness includes recognizing and embracing the defects and vulnerabilities of existence with generosity and understanding, instead of taking a stab at flawlessness or unforgiving self-judgment.

Start by rehearsing self-sympathy, which includes treating yourself with the very level of benevolence and understanding that you would propose to a dear companion confronting comparative difficulties. Perceive that you are just human, and that it's normal to experience challenges, difficulties, and snapshots of battle en route. Rather than scolding yourself for saw disappointments or weaknesses, offer yourself inspirational statements, backing, and graciousness, perceiving that you are doing all that can be expected with the assets and information you have.

Besides, embrace acknowledgment for the excursion you have voyaged - including both the victories and the difficulties. Relinquish the requirement for things to be great or for your excursion to unfurl precisely as expected, and on second thought embrace the inborn chaos and unconventionality of life. Perceive that difficulties and hindrances are a characteristic piece of the excursion, and that they offer significant open doors for development, learning, and self-revelation.

Furthermore, let go of the need to contrast yourself with others or to stick to outside principles of progress or accomplishment. Embrace your uniqueness and singularity, perceiving that your process is interestingly yours and that you are on your own way toward satisfaction and development. Trust in your own insight and instinct, and have confidence in your capacity to explore life's difficulties with beauty, strength, and boldness.

As you embrace self-sympathy and acknowledgment, make sure to rehearse persistence and delicacy with yourself as you explore the highs and lows of the excursion. Develop a feeling of interest and transparency toward yourself and your encounters, permitting yourself to gain and develop from every second, whether or not it's a snapshot of progress or disappointment.

At last, embracing self-empathy and acknowledgment is tied in with embracing yourself - blemishes, defects, and all - with unqualified love and thoughtfulness. By treating yourself with sympathy and acknowledgment, you make an underpinning of internal strength and versatility that permits you to explore life's difficulties with beauty and credibility. In this way, set out to embrace self-sympathy and acknowledgment as fundamental colleagues on your excursion toward deliberate living, realizing that inside their hug lies the way to opening an existence of genuine satisfaction, reason, and importance.

Respecting Your Credibility and Truth

Vital to living with purposefulness is the demonstration of respecting your realness and truth - embracing who you are at your center and living in arrangement with your most profound qualities, goals, and convictions. As you praise your excursion toward purposeful living, pause for a minute to perceive and respect the boldness it takes to live legitimately in a world that frequently compels us to adjust to outer assumptions and standards.

Start by recognizing the exceptional characteristics, gifts, and abilities that make you what your identity is. Think about the qualities, interests, and interests that are generally critical to you, and consider how you can respect and communicate them genuinely in your day to day existence. Embrace your uniqueness and singularity, perceiving that your genuineness is your most prominent strength and a wellspring of strengthening and satisfaction.

Additionally, praise the excursion of self-revelation and self-articulation that has carried you to this second. Perceive the breakthrough moments, understanding, and mindfulness that have permitted you to reveal your actual self and live in arrangement with your qualities and yearnings. Embrace the course of development and change, realizing that each step you take toward credibility carries you more like an existence of genuine satisfaction and significance.

Furthermore, honor the mental fortitude it takes to live legitimately in a world that frequently esteems similarity over distinction. Embrace weakness and straightforwardness in your connections and communications, permitting yourself to be perceived the truth about and heard. Trust in your own instinct and inward insight, and have confidence in the legitimacy of your own encounters and bits of insight.

As you honor your legitimacy and truth, make sure to be delicate and caring with yourself en route. Embrace the defects and weaknesses that make you human, and permit yourself the opportunity to commit errors and gain from them. Trust in the excursion of self-disclosure and development, knowing that every second - whether it's a snapshot of progress or disappointment - is a potential chance to extend your association with your actual self.

At last, regarding your legitimacy and truth is tied in with embracing the totality of what your identity is and living with trustworthiness, mental fortitude, and conviction. By regarding your credibility, you make a day to day existence that is profoundly lined up with your qualities and desires, and you enable yourself to live with reason, energy, and importance. In this way, try to respect your validness and truth as you commend your excursion toward purposeful living, realizing that inside their hug lies the way to opening an existence of genuine satisfaction and credibility.

Developing a Feeling of Festivity

As you approach the climax of your excursion toward purposeful living, develop a feeling of festivity that implants every second with delight, appreciation, and satisfaction. Festivity is a strong practice that permits us to respect the achievements, accomplishments, and encounters that have enhanced our lives and carried us nearer to our objectives and desires. By embracing the soul of festivity, we recognize the excellence and extravagance of life and develop a profound feeling of appreciation for the actual excursion.

Start by perceiving the meaning of festivity as an approach to denoting the achievements and accomplishments along your excursion. Carve out opportunity to recognize and commend the headway you've made, the objectives you've accomplished, and the development you've encountered. Whether it's a little triumph or a significant achievement, every achievement deserve festivity and fills in as a sign of your strength, assurance, and obligation to living with deliberateness.

Besides, develop a feeling of appreciation and appreciation for the actual excursion - including both the ups and the downs, the delights and the difficulties. Ponder the encounters, valuable open doors, and examples advanced en route, and offer ardent thanks for the wealth and overflow they have brought to your life. By commending the excursion with appreciation, you develop a feeling of overflow and satisfaction that enhances each part of your life.

Moreover, commend individuals who play had an impact in your excursion - the companions, relatives, tutors, and partners who have upheld you, empowered you, and rooted for you en route. Express genuine appreciation for their presence in your life and the manners by which they have added to your development and prosperity. Commend their accomplishments, achievements, and triumphs also, realizing that your process is interwoven with theirs.

Moreover, develop a feeling of festivity in your everyday existence, tracking down happiness and satisfaction right now. Get some margin to relish the straightforward delights of life - whether it's partaking in a flavorful feast, investing energy in nature, or imparting chuckling to friends and family. Praise the snapshots of association, motivation, and ponder that give light and pleasure into your life, realizing that every second is a gift to be valued and celebrated.

At last, developing a feeling of festivity is tied in with embracing the excellence, extravagance, and intricacy of existence with great enthusiasm and a thankful heart. By commending the achievements, accomplishments, and encounters along your excursion, you honor the strength, fortitude, and responsibility it takes to live with purposeful-ness. Thus, try to embrace the soul of festivity as you mark the finish of your excursion toward deliberate living, realizing that inside its hug lies the way to opening an existence of genuine satisfaction, reason, and delight.

Conclusion: The Continuing Path of Purposeful Living

Pondering Illustrations Learned

As you finish up your excursion of deliberate living, it's fundamental to require investment for thoughtfulness and reflection on the important examples advanced en route. Considering your encounters permits you to acquire knowledge into the different difficulties, wins, and snapshots of development that have molded your way. Consider the impediments you've experienced and the methodologies you've utilized to defeat them. Consider the breakthrough moments and motivation that have directed you toward a more profound comprehension of your motivation and values. By considering the illustrations learned, you gain a more profound appreciation for the excursion you've embraced and the insight acquired en route. These bits of knowledge act as important guideposts as you forge ahead with your way of deliberate living, illuminating your choices and activities with clearness, expectation, and insight.

Focusing on Long lasting Development and Improvement

As you arrive at the finish of your excursion of intentional living, it's vital to perceive that the mission for self-awareness and advancement is a continuous undertaking. Focusing on deep rooted learning and personal development is fundamental for keeping up with energy and remaining lined up with your motivation and values. Embrace the outlook of constant development and advancement, understanding that each new experience offers a chance for learning and self-disclosure.

Promise to persistently extend your points of view and challenge yourself to step beyond your usual range of familiarity. Search out new open doors for learning and development, whether through conventional schooling, individual investigation, or active encounters. Develop a feeling of interest and receptiveness to novel thoughts, viewpoints, and potential outcomes, perceiving that development frequently happens when we embrace the obscure and wander into an unfamiliar area.

Additionally, focus on creating yourself mentally as well as inwardly, profoundly, and truly. Take part in rehearses that sustain your brain, body, and soul, like contemplation, work out, imaginative articulation, and profound investigation. Develop propensities and schedules that help your general prosperity and add to your development and improvement all in all individual.

Besides, embrace difficulties and mishaps as any open doors for development and strength. Comprehend that mishaps are a characteristic piece of the excursion and proposition important examples and experiences that can assist you with developing further and stronger notwithstanding difficulty. Move toward difficulties with a development outlook, seeing them as any open doors to learn, adjust, and advance.

By focusing on deep rooted development and improvement, you guarantee that your excursion of intentional living remaining parts dynamic, satisfying, and significant. Embrace the excursion with energy, interest, and a readiness to develop and grow your points of view ceaselessly. As you set out on this long lasting journey for development and self-revelation, realize that each step you take carries you more like an existence of genuine satisfaction, reason, and significance.

Developing Flexibility Notwithstanding Affliction

As you close your excursion of deliberate living, it's pivotal to perceive the significance of developing versatility notwithstanding misfortune. Over the course of life, you will unavoidably experience difficulties, misfortunes, and snags that test your purpose and assurance. Developing flexibility permits you to explore these difficulties with fortitude, strength, and tirelessness, guaranteeing that you stay lined up with your motivation and values even amidst difficulty.

Recognize that misfortunes and snags are a characteristic piece of the human experience and an inescapable part of seeking after an existence of direction and significance. Rather than review difficulties as outlandish hindrances, move toward them with an outlook of flexibility - a faith in your capacity to quickly return from difficulty more grounded and stronger than previously.

Develop flexibility by taking on sound methods for dealing with especially difficult times and methodologies for overseeing pressure and affliction. Practice taking care of oneself and self-sympathy, focusing on your physical, profound, and mental prosperity. Take part in exercises that support your spirit and recharge your energy, like investing time in nature, rehearsing care, or associating with friends and family.

In addition, embrace difficulties as any open doors for development and self-revelation. Perceive that every difficulty offers significant examples and bits of knowledge that can assist you with developing further and stronger over the long haul. Move toward difficulties with a feeling of interest and receptiveness, seeing them as any open doors to learn, adjust, and develop personally.

Rest on your encouraging group of people for direction, consolation, and basic reassurance during troublesome times. Encircle yourself with companions, relatives, tutors, and partners who can offer viewpoint, intelligence, and a listening ear when you want it most. Recollect that you don't need to confront difficulties alone and that looking for help is an indication of solidarity, not shortcoming.

By developing flexibility notwithstanding affliction, you engage yourself to remain consistent with your motivation and values in any event, whenever difficulties arise. Embrace difficulties as any open doors for development, rest on your encouraging group of people for direction and support, and practice taking care of oneself and self-sympathy to feed your spirit and recharge your energy. As you develop versatility, realize that you have the strength and boldness to beat any snag that hinders you, guaranteeing that your excursion of intentional living remaining parts lively, satisfying, and profoundly significant.

Sustaining Association and Local area

As you close your excursion of deliberate living, perceive the important job that association and local area play in supporting and advancing your way. Developing significant connections and cultivating a feeling of having a place are fundamental components of carrying on with a reason driven life. Embrace the force of association with help you in the midst of hardship, to praise your victories, and to develop how you might interpret yourself and your general surroundings.

Put investment into sustaining your associations with the individuals who share your qualities and desires. Encircle yourself with people who elevate and rouse you, who challenge you to develop and advance, and who offer immovable help and support on your excursion. Develop genuine associations in light of shared regard, trust, and weakness, realizing that the bonds you structure with others are a wellspring of solidarity and flexibility.

Moreover, effectively draw in with your local area - whether it's your nearby area, work environment, or interpersonal organization - and add to its development and prosperity. Search out valuable chances to offer in return and have a beneficial outcome on the existences of others, whether through chipping in, tutoring, or thoughtful gestures. By supporting association and local area, you not just improve the existences of everyone around you yet additionally develop your own feeling of direction and satisfaction.

Rest on your encouraging group of people for direction, support, and friendship as you explore the difficulties and wins of life. Share your fantasies, fears, and desires with confided in companions and guides, realizing that they will give point of view, shrewdness, and compassion consequently. Praise your victories together and draw strength from each other during seasons of trouble, realizing that you are never alone on your excursion.

Additionally, embrace the variety and lavishness of human experience by drawing in with people from various foundations, societies, and viewpoints. Listen profoundly to the narratives and encounters of others, looking to comprehend and relate to their remarkable points of view and battles. By embracing variety and consideration, you enhance your comprehension own might interpret the world and develop a more extensive feeling of sympathy and compassion for mankind in general.

All in all, sustaining association and local area is fundamental for carrying on with a reason driven life that is profoundly satisfying and significant. Embrace the force of valid connections, effectively draw in with your local area, and rest on your encouraging group of people for direction and support. By developing association and local area, you make an underpinning of solidarity and flexibility that supports you on your excursion of intentional living and enhances the existences of people around you.

Embracing the Excursion with Satisfaction and Appreciation

As you arrive at the finish of your excursion of deliberate living, embrace the way forward with a feeling of euphoria, appreciation, and appreciation for the wealth and excellence of life. Developing an outlook of appreciation permits you to perceive the overflow and favors that encompass you every day, cultivating a profound feeling of satisfaction and satisfaction right now.

Move toward every day with a thankful heart, finding opportunity to recognize and value the straightforward delights and delights that enhance your life - whether it's the glow of the sun all over, the giggling of friends and family, or the magnificence of nature surrounding you. By developing appreciation for the current second, you implant every day with a feeling of marvel and appreciation that upgrades your general prosperity and enhances your experience of life.

Besides, offer thanks for the actual excursion - the difficulties, wins, and snapshots of development that have molded you into the individual you are today. Think about the examples took in, the bits of knowledge acquired, and the insight gained en route, perceiving the worth of each involvement with adding to your self-improvement and advancement.

Commend your triumphs and achievements with a thankful heart, perceiving the difficult work, devotion, and constancy that have carried you to this point. Set aside some margin to respect and value the help of the people who have went with you on your excursion - the companions, relatives, coaches, and partners who have given a shout out to you, offered direction and support, and partook in your victories and difficulties.

Besides, move toward the future with positive thinking and expectation, realizing that each new day offers a new chance for development, disclosure, and satisfaction. Embrace the obscure with interest and receptiveness, confiding in the excursion and the insight of your own instinct to direct you forward.

All in all, embrace the excursion of deliberate living with bliss, appreciation, and appreciation for the lavishness and magnificence of life. Develop a mentality of appreciation for the current second and the actual excursion, praising every day as a gift and each experience as a chance for development and self-disclosure. By embracing the excursion with delight and appreciation, you make a daily existence that is lively, satisfying, and profoundly significant, knowing that inside the hug of intentional living untruths the way to opening an existence of genuine bliss and satisfaction.